The Handbook of Horse Breeds

The Handbook of Horse Breeds

Maria Costantino

BARNES & NOBLE BOOKS

NEW YORK

This edition published by Barnes & Noble, Inc.,
By arrangement with D&S Books Ltd

2004 Barnes & Noble Books

M   10   9   8   7   6   5   4   3   2

ISBN 0-7607-5659-7

Creative Director: Sarah King
Editor: Anna Southgate
Project Editor: Judith Millidge
Photographer: Paul Forrester
Designer: Axis Design

© 2003 D&S Books Ltd

Printed in China

Contents

Introduction

Equine Evolution

It could be argued that no other living creature has had the same cultural effect on the civilizations of man as the horse. For centuries, horses carried kings and emperors into battle and helped govern the destinies of empires. The horse was also man's first source of power combined with speed and, until relatively recently in Europe and America when mechanization took command, the horse was the most efficient method of transport on land.

While the horse has been associated with man for 4,000 years, this is in fact only a tiny part of the horse's history, which can be traced back some 75 million years to the now extinct family of Condylarth, a prehistoric group of animals which varied in size from a cat to a medium-sized dog. The condylarths had five toes on each foot and at the end of each toe was a thickened nail. While these animals were not horses, they were the ancestors of them and all hoofed animals.

Our modern horse, *Equus caballus*, is the direct descendant of a small animal which flourished about 60 million years ago, called Eohippus, the 'Dawn Horse'. The difference between the Dawn Horse and the modern horse were so great that when in 1839 archaeologists found the fossil remains of Eohippus at Studd Hill in Kent, England, they identified it incorrectly as belonging to Hyrax, a genus of rabbit-like mammals.

This was not surprising since the Studd Hill remains had four toes on each forefoot and three on each hind foot, and, the toes

THE MODERN HORSE DIFFERS GREATLY FROM ITS ORIGINAL ANCESTOR, EOHIPPUS.

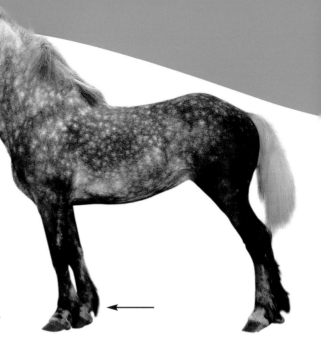

THE ERGOT IS THE ONLY REMAINDER OF THE PAD FEATURED ON EOHIPPUS.

ended in a miniature hoof rather than a dog's claw although each foot had a pad like a dog's which carried most of the animal's weight. In fact, this pad does persist on the modern horse in the form of the ergot, a small horny growth on the back of the fetlock joint. Furthermore, the Studd Hill animal's teeth were short-crowned molars, like those of monkeys or pigs, not designed for grazing grass, but for nibbling at shrubs.

In 1876, scientists unearthed a nearly complete skeleton in the Eocene rock formations in Wyoming, U.S.A. and this was correctly identified as Eohippus, the ancestor of our modern horse. In 1931, in the Big Horn Basin in Wyoming, scientists discovered another near complete skeleton of Eohippus. This skeleton was reconstructed, and along with the evidence offered by the other remains, provides the most accurate representation of the Dawn Horse. The Big Horn Eohippus stood almost 14 inches high at the shoulder and would have weighed approximately 12 pounds.

The following year, in 1932, Sir Clive Foster-Cooper realized that the Studd Hill fossils and those of Eohippus were so similar that the British remains did, in fact, belong to the European variety of Eohippus. Sixty million years ago, sea levels were much lower than those today and there were land bridges across what is now the Bering Strait between Asia and North America; across the Mediterranean from Italy and the Iberian Peninsula to North Africa, and across the English Channel. Consequently, Eohippus and its descendants could roam freely throughout Europe, America, and Asia, adapting and evolving depending on the climate and landscape in which it lived: the smallest Eohippus may have been no more than 10 inches tall at the shoulder, some may have been twice that size, and it is possible that much bigger types existed in Europe.

The next significant development in the evolution of the horse occurred during the

Oligocene period, around 35-40 million years ago. During this time the descendants of Eohippus gradually became more like today's horses. Mesohippus was a little taller, standing about 18 inches high on longer legs. They also now had three toes on each foot, with the central toe on each more elongated. This indicates that since more weight was being carried on the middle toe, the ground on which the Mesohippus was living was much firmer. Their skulls also began to develop premolar, incisor teeth, better designed for eating a greater range of vegetation now prevalent, as the jungle habitats common at the time of Eohippus were giving way to more wooded, scrublands.

As the changes in climate, terrain and vegetation continued over the next 15 million years, and the jungle gave way first to temperate woodlands and then to treeless, grassy plains, the 'equus' evolved and adapted to their new environment in a classic demonstration of evolution's 'survival of the fittest'. Mesohippus was succeeded by the slightly larger Miohippus, and then by Parahippus. The rounded arched backs of the earlier 'horses' had now disappeared and longer legs increased the animal's speed over the now open ground in which they lived.

Around 25-20 million years ago, another development occurred in the evolution of the horse: Merychippus, which was taller, measuring up to 36 inches at the shoulder. This animal was still three-toed, but the central toe was increasingly bearing the animal's weight and the outside toes were becoming diminished in size and function. With a longer neck – which enabled it to feed at ground level and raise its head to increase its range of vision – and higher crowned teeth covered in a stronger, more protective enamel more suited to grazing harder grasses, Merychippus was more recognizably a horse – although it was not the 'prototype' for modern Equus.

The 'true' horse would develop from Pliohippus which emerged in the mid-Pleistocene period, about 6 million years ago. Standing about 48 inches at the shoulder, Pliohippus had the general proportions of the modern horse and was the first to have a single hoof. Pliohippus was also to be the source for the sub-group of animals which includes zebras, domestic and wild asses, and the hemionids (the 'half-asses' such as Onagers, Mongolian Kulans, the Indian Ghorkar and the Tibetan Kiang).

The First True Horse

About five million years later, during the second half of the Ice Age, the first 'true' horse, *Equus caballus* emerged ('caballine' means 'of or belonging to horses'). *Equus caballus* varied in size, but was commonly about the height of a small, island-bred Shetland Pony and probably just as shaggy.

For the first quarter of a million years of its existence, *Equus caballus* could travel freely from its birthplace in North America across the land bridges to Asia, to Europe

PRZEWALSKI'S WILD HORSE IS BELIEVED TO BE ONE OF THE THREE ANCESTORS OF TODAY'S MODERN HORSES.

THE FIRST 'TRUE HORSE' PROBABLY LOOKED SIMILAR TO TODAY'S SHETLAND PONY.

and to Africa as its ancestors had also done. Gradually they were being driven south in search of grazing lands as the ice sheets advanced (and retreated at least four times over a period of about 600,000 years). Around 9000 BC the land bridge across the Bering Strait disappeared with the recession and melting of the last ice sheet, and the continent of America was left isolated from Europe and Asia. Some 8,000 years ago the horse – along with the mastodons – became totally extinct in America and the equine species would not be introduced again into the Americas until the 16th century with the arrival of the

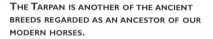

Spanish conquistadors when Hernan
Cortés (1485-1547) arrived in Mexico with
16 horses in 1519.

The land bridges between Britain and the
Continent and between Europe and Africa
also became submerged: since then, apart by
the intervention of man, no horse crossed
from Europe in the British Isles. When the ice
sheets had finally retreated to their present
positions, just over 10,000 years ago, only
four groups of the descendants of Eohippus
remained alive: the horse in Europe and
western Asia; asses in northern Africa; zebras
in southern and eastern Africa; and onagers
in the Middle East.

The terrain of Europe and western Asia
which contained horses comprises various
regions which differ significantly in altitude
and climate. These factors would inevitably
have affected the horses and ponies which
developed in them. Temperate climates and
moderate altitudes promoted greater size in
horses, while very high altitudes and
extremes in climate tend to encourage the
development of ponies rather than horses.
Different soil types would have produced
different types of grasses which varied in
mineral and vitamin content: while areas
with heavy rainfall – resulting in rich, lush
pastures – tended to produce heavier

**THE TARPAN IS ANOTHER OF THE ANCIENT
BREEDS REGARDED AS AN ANCESTOR OF OUR
MODERN HORSES.**

horses, and more arid regions with sparser
grazing, produced lighter, faster-moving
animals.

By the end of the Ice Age there were four
types of primitive horses to be found – three
of which are now regarded as the ancestors
of our modern breeds: the Forest Horse;
Przewalski's Asiatic Wild Horse; the Tarpan,
or, desert/plateau horse, and the Tundra
horse of northeastern Siberia. This last, now
extinct horse type, is thought by some to be
the ancestor of the modern Yakut pony,
while others consider it a derivative of the
Asiatic Wild Horse. Nevertheless, there is a
general consensus that the Tundra horse
had no real influence on equine
development south of the Arctic Circle.

11

REMAINS OF THE FOREST HORSE SUGGEST A RELATIONSHIP WITH TODAY'S SWEDISH HEAVY HORSE.

The Forest Horse

Knowledge of *Equus caballus silvaticus*, the Forest or Diluvial horse, is based on evidence from excavations around Dummer Lake in northwest Germany, of a heavy breed of wild horse which existed in Scandinavia nearly 10,000 years ago. This horse had a massive body and a passive temperament, acquired from grazing lush European pastures and was being domesticated around 3,000 years ago. At Lake Dummer, three types of remains were found: the most common remains of horses were pony-sized animals, possibly a native wild horse that seems to have been hunted for food. The other two were domesticated Forest Horses. One was an intermediate size, while the other was a large, heavy horse that may have been related to the Swedish Heavy Horse. Further archaeological evidence of the Forest Horse was found in cave drawings at Cambrelles in the Dordogne, France which date from after the glacial period.

Przewalski's Asiatic Wild Horse

Of the four varieties that existed at the end of the Ice Age, the Asiatic Wild Horse is the only surviving member of the 'primitive' trio of horse ancestors that exists today and is the only true 'wild' horse. *Equus caballus Przewalskii Przewalskii Poliakov*, to give it its scientific name, is also known as the Taki in Mongolia and as the Kertag among the people of Kyrghyz. In 1879, a herd of wild horse were 'rediscovered' in the Central Asian steppes by the Russian explorer, Colonel Nikolai Mikhailovitch Przewalski (1839-88) and cataloged in 1881 by the zoologist J.S. Poliakov. These horses differed from domesticated horses in a number of ways, including the fact that they had erect manes. Compact and generally dun-colored, with a narrow, dark dorsal stripe and occasional faint leg stripes, the adults varied between 12 and 14 hands high (average 4 ft high). These Asiatic Wild Horses are now believed to form part of the foundation stock from which sprang the ancestors of the Arabian and other Eastern horses, and, although they are far removed, they are ancestors of our modern Thoroughbreds.

The Tarpan
(Desert/Plateau Horse)

The original home of this horse type, *Equus caballus gmelini*, was farther west than Przewalski's Horse, in the southern steppes of Russia. There also seem to have been two types of these wild, primitive horses: one grazing on the steppes of the Ukraine, and the other in eastern Europe. Both were hunted because the wild stallions attacked and often killed their domesticated rivals. They were first observed scientifically in the 18th century by Antonius Gmelin, a German-Russian scientist but were named by zoologist Otto Antonius later in the 19th century. By this time, both branches of the Tarpan family had been mated with domesticated horses, and the remaining wild examples had been hunted to near extinction. Although the last wild Tarpan died at Askania Nova (in the south of the Ukraine in the Crimea) in 1880, steps had been taken to preserve – or restore – the breed. Today a reconstituted herd, back-bred from Tarpan-related stock survives in a semi-wild state in the forest reserves of Bialowieza and Polielno in Poland and is used for experimental breeding. A strong influence on light horse stock, the Tarpan

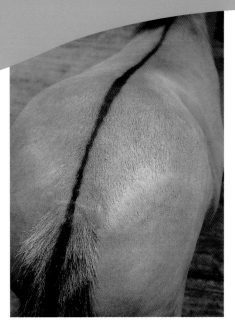

THE DORSAL STRIPE IS ONE OF THE TARPAN'S DISTINGUISHING FEATURES.

are about the same size as Przewalski's Horse and are generally brown in color with a dorsal stripe, black mane and tail. It is now generally believed that the Tarpan and Przewalski's Horse are the joint ancestors of today's warmblood breeds. This term refers not to a horse's body temperature, but to the presence of Thoroughbred or Eastern blood, while heavy draught horses, on the other hand, are generally reckoned to be descended from cold blood stock of the primitive Forest Horse.

Secondary Foundation Lines:
The Theory of Four Basic Horse Types

The theory of four post-glacial horse types which originated in crosses of the Tarpan, Przewalski's Asiatic Wild Horse and the Forest Horse and their offspring and which took place in Eurasia some 5-6,000 years ago, was first postulated by J.G. Speed of Edinburgh, E. Skorkowski of Cracow, Poland, F. Ebhardt of Stuttgart, Germany, and, R. d'Andrade of Portugal, all acknowledged experts in the field of equine prehistory. The 'Speed Group' suggested that four types of horse had evolved by the time domestication was taking place: Pony Type 1 and Pony Type 2; Horse Type 3 and Horse Type 4.

According to the Speed Group, Pony Type 1 evolved from the Tarpan and averaged 48-50 in.(12-12.2 hh) and was brown or bay in color. This pony became established in northwest Europe and was a sturdy animal, resistant to the wet conditions and cold winds of the region in which it lived. The nearest modern equivalents to Pony Type 1, which also share their ancestors' resilience, are the Exmoor ponies.

Pony Type 2 was a more heavily built and slightly larger animal, standing between 56-58 in. (14-14.2 hh) which lived in northern Eurasia. This animal had a more convex profile on a heavy head, was dun-colored ranging to yellow, and had a pronounced eel, or dorsal stripe. In appearance it resembled Przewalski's Asiatic Wild Horse, but it did not share the same hereditary characteristics passed on in the chromosomes: the Asiatic Wild Horse has 66 chromosomes, while the Pony Type 2 had 64, like the modern domestic horse. The modern equivalents of Pony Type 2 are

ONE OF TODAY'S EQUIVALENTS OF PONY TYPE 3 IS THE AKHAL-TEKE.

the Highland Pony, the Norwegian Fjord, and the Noriker – although this breed was also influenced by the primitive Forest Horse.

Horse Type 3, according to the Speed Group, was a desert horse, well adapted to a harsh environment: it would have been a horse with a spare frame, thin skin and an ultra fine coat enabling it to withstand heat and drought. This horse stood about 60in (14.3 hh), with a long, narrow body, long neck, and ears, with broad shallow feet to withstand soft, sandy terrain. Horse Type 3's habitat was Central Asia, but it also extended westward into Spain and its modern-day

equivalents are the Akhal-Teke of the Turkmenistan desert and the Sorraia of Portugal and Spain.

The final horse type, Type 4, was smaller in stature, standing about 48 in. high (12 hh) and was more 'refined' than Type 3 with a straighter profile, and a silky, fine mane, tail and body hair. Native to western Asia, it was also 'heat resistant'. The influence on this horse is more Tarpan than Asiatic Wild Horse, and Horse Type 4 is often proposed as the prototype Arab, with the Caspian as its nearest modern equivalent.

THE CASPIAN IS REGARDED AS THE NEAREST MODERN EQUIVALENT OF PONY TYPE 4.

Chapter 1
Domestication and the Modern Horse

The domestication of horses introduced human intervention into what had previously been a natural development of the species, a development governed by the ability of those best suited to survive and adapt to changing circumstances. The modern horse is thus the product of selective breeding, and, with human intervention, equine evolution was speeded up.

The earliest written reference to the horse came from China, where, approximately 4,300 years ago, a scribe reported raids by nomad horsemen. Beyond China, of the three great civilizations at the time, in Mesopotamia, in the Indus Valley (in what is now Pakistan) and in Egypt, none had any knowledge of horses until about 4,000 years ago when a scribe in Ur of the Chaldees reported what was to him a new kind of animal which he called the "ass from the mountains".

When Egypt was invaded around 3,700 years ago by warriors in horse-drawn chariots, this was the Egyptians' first experience of both the horse and the wheel. Shortly after the invasion of Egypt, the Hittite charioteers captured the supposedly invincible city of Babylon. Just 100 years later, the Indus valley civilization was also conquered by barbarians on horseback. In

less than 300 years, the three greatest civilizations were destroyed because of the mobility given to the victors by their horses.

The Hittites were among the first people to produce a manual with precise details for 'training and acclimatization' of horses in Turkey. This manual was written by a Mittanian horse dealer called Kikkuli in about 1360 BC and he advised the feeding of grain and chaffed straw at regulated times to synchronize with exercise in order to maximize a horse's fitness and stamina.

The earliest horse breeders of whom we have any detailed knowledge, however, were the ancient Assyrians. Their horses appear to have lacked stamina at first as their art reveals that mounted warriors needed to lead a spare horse. Gradually though, bigger and more powerful horses were bred which could not only carry a man, but all his weapons and armor too. The first recorded successful breeders of weight-carrying chargers were the Persians, who by the 6th century BC had wrested power and supremacy from the Assyrians and were the dominant power in the east. Central to their success was the Nisean horse, the exact origins of which are unknown. The Tarpan, along with Horse Type 4, both lived in the same region and there may also have been out-crosses with the Asiatic Wild Horse to produce the Nisean horse that was bigger than any other horse used before, measuring 60 in. (15 hh) and possibly more. These magnificent horses were said to have had 'feet that shake the earth'.

In Persian religious beliefs the horse also played a role: Mithras, the god of light and the 'lord of wide pastures' was believed to ride a chariot drawn by four immortal, white horses, shod with gold and fed on ambrosia.

For more than 300 years the Persian Empire was the greatest force in the ancient world, but even they were to come under threat from nomadic horsemen, the Scythians and Parthians. Expert horsemen and archers, capable of firing while riding at full gallop, it was the Parthians who gave us the term 'parting shot'. More correctly though, it was the 'Parthian shot': riding away from their enemy, the Parthians would turn around in the saddle and loose a final arrow over their mount's tail.

The Greeks and the Romans were not the same caliber of horsemen as the Scythians or Parthians, but both empires nevertheless relied on horse power to extend their power. The Greeks left a legacy of

horsemanship in the form of *The Cavalry Commander*, a manual written by the soldier, philosopher, and historian Xenophon (c. 430-356 BC) in which he described how mounted Greek soldiers were employed to scout in advance of the main body of the army and harass the enemy by launching javelins at their foot soldiers.

The climate and thin soil of Greece was not ideal horse breeding ground, however, and most horses were imported from Ferghana (southern Russia) in the east to be crossed with the Greeks' own stock from Thessaly. To increase their size, Philip of Macedon imported some 20,000 Scythian mares and legend has it that in 343 BC he bought his son, Alexander the Great (356-323 BC), the great horse called Bucephalus for the equivalent of $40,000. The name Bucephalus means 'ox head', and refers to the broad forehead and concave profile characteristic of a particular Thessalonian breed. Bucephalus had a black coat, a white star on his forehead, and according to some, blue eyes. He was also unruly and could not be mounted until Alexander realized that the horse was afraid of his own shadow and those cast by anyone who approached him. Alexander turned

Bucephalus to face the sun, mounted and rode the great horse. In 333 BC Alexander, riding Bucephalus, led the Greeks to victory against the Persians under Darius. In 327 BC, Alexander rode Bucephalus for the last time when the Greeks defeated the Indian king Porus at the Hydaspes River. Bucephalus, now 30 years old, was wounded in battle, and when he died, he was buried with full military honors.

Horses occupied a central role in Greek religious beliefs: although he was the god of the sea, Poseidon was credited with the creation of the horse. Naturally, Ares, the god of war, rode in a chariot drawn by the now obligatory four white horses, while Demeter, goddess of women and agriculture, was depicted with the head of a black mare. The most famous horse of Greek mythology is undoubtedly the winged horse, Pegasus. Born of the blood of the Medusa when she was killed by Perseus, Pegasus was caught by Bellerophon while he was drinking at the spring of Pirene – which can still be seen in the ruins of old Corinth, Greece. Beloved by the Muses for creating the spring Hippocrene on Mount Helicon by a stamp of his magic hoof, Pegasus later became a symbol for immortality and for flights of the

imagination. During World War Two, Pegasus, with Bellerophon on his back was the insignia of all British Airborne troops.

Although chariot racing was popular and horses were in general use, the Romans in battle relied more on the mighty strength of their legions of foot soldiers. Nevertheless, Roman breeders did produce stock for a wide range of purposes, including circus and parade horses, draft and harness horses, hunters, and race horses. Although draft animals were in constant supply to transport military provisions it was not until the Punic Wars (264-149 BC) that the Romans realized the need for cavalry, and Iberia (Spain and Portugal) became the principle center for breeding cavalry horses. Mounted troops were vital to military success, as Julius Caesar would find when his first attempt to invade Britain in 55 BC failed because his mounted divisions did not arrive in time. Although Caesar had better luck though the following year, it was not until the reigns of Diocletian (284-305) and later Constantine (311-37) that the Romans really developed their cavalry and mounted divisions were divided into *clibanarii* (light cavalry) and *catafracti* (heavy horsemen). But even these were no match for the Hun archers who rode with stirrups and saddles which they used as platforms from which they fired their arrows. In 378 the Roman legions faced the massed horse of the Goths and Huns at Adrianople, a battle which would mark the beginning of the end of the Roman Empire and the rise of heavy cavalry in Europe.

The two northern European nations, the Goths and the Vandals produced heavy weight chargers, no doubt the product of breeding from the heavy Forest horses of Scandinavia and northern Germany. The Goths fought their way across Europe from their homelands around the Baltic to southern Russia, while the heavy horses of the Vandals carried them victoriously from northern Germany, down through southern Europe and across the narrow Straits of Gibraltar into North Africa, where during their century of occupation, their cold-blooded horses left their imprint on native horse breeds. A third Germanic nation emerged 100 years later: the Lombards. By this time, their heavy chargers were ridden with stirrups newly introduced from the east, which enabled the Lombard cavaliers to employ a mighty lance called a *contus* as they rode south into Italy.

Around the same time in the east, riding horses were being bred in Syria and Palestine, but it was not until the 6th century AD with the influence of the Prophet Muhammad (570-632) that the breeding and owning of horses became significant. Horses now provided the means by which Islam could be spread and it is said that Islam was founded on the 'hoof prints of the Arabian horse'.

Following the Prophet's death, the Moslem armies under Abubekr, expanded beyond the desert lands of the Middle East. Just ten years later, most of the Christian Byzantine Empire had fallen to the armies of Islam which now controlled Syria, Palestine, Mesopotamia (modern Iran) and Armenia. By 643 all of North Africa was under their control and the following year the Indus Valley (in present day Pakistan) was occupied. By the beginning of the 8th century, Islam had claimed Central Asia and the Moors of North Africa had crossed into Spain where in 711 AD, they defeated Roderic, the last Visigoth king before advancing over the Pyrenees into Gaul (France).

In 732 the armies of Islam were halted at Poitiers by Charles Martel and his Frankish knights and the Moors pushed back into Spain. Although they were to occupy the area for the next 700 years, they never advanced further into Europe.

During the Crusades, the many military engagements between the armies of Christian Europe and the Moslem east, captured Eastern stallions were brought back to Europe. These nations realized that success in future wars was greatly dependent on the quality of their horses, and from then on, horse breeding was practised systematically in almost every country, often under royal patronage. The eastern horses, in particular the Arab, the Barb, and the Barb's offshoot, the Spanish horse, were to become the foundation stock for the Thoroughbred, as well as all the world's light horse breeds.

The Arab and the Barb

The Arabian horse is considered as the purest of all breeds and there is evidence that the breed was in existence at least 4,500 years ago around the Arabian Peninsula where the geography of the region, coupled with the climate of the desert, ensured the purity of the Arab's blood. The nomadic Bedu tribes of the desert trace the line back to the mare Baz, who was said to have been captured in the Yemen by the great-great grandson of Noah, and the stallion Hoshaba.

The Barb is a North African horse which was introduced into Europe in the 8th century. Completely different in both character and appearance from the Arab, despite crossings with Arab stock, the Barb remained genetically dominant and had a significant effect on European and American breeds, since it was 'perpetuated' by the Spanish horse of the 16th and 17th centuries. Spanish blood is evident throughout the warmblood horses of Europe: in Lipizzaners and Cleveland Bays as well as Highland Ponies and Welsh Cobs.

THE ARAB IS CONSIDERED TO BE THE PUREST OF ALL MODERN HORSE BREEDS.

The Ancestors of the Thoroughbred

The Thoroughbred first evolved in England in the 17th and 18th centuries to satisfy the needs of royalty and the nobility for horse racing. Eastern blood had been introduced some time before: returning Crusaders had brought back eastern stallions as booty during the Crusades, and King Richard I was even presented with some stallions by his Moslem opponent, the mighty Saladin. British horses at the time were still not much over 13 hh and King Henry VIII — who in full armor weighed in at a very hefty 30 stone (520 lb) — expressed fears that the breed of good strong horses might die out. Accordingly, he decreed that land owners must keep herds of breeding mares over 13 'handfuls' in height. He also prohibited the use of stallions of less than 15 'handfuls', while every archbishop and duke had to maintain seven 'trotting stone horses for the saddle', each of which was to measure no less than 14 hh when three years old.

Thomas Blundeville's 16th century book, *The Fower Chiefyst Offices Belongyng to Horsemanshippe*, lists the breeds of horses known in Britain around 1550: he begins his list with the 'Turke' which he described as 'very swift in their running and of great courage'. Blundeville goes on to state that all the horses which came from the Turk's domains should be called Turkey Horses. Much of Arabia, as well as Syria, was at this time part of the Turkish Empire and Turkey controlled much of the coast of the Mediterranean from Greece to the Lebanon, Israel, Egypt and Libya. Consequently any Arabian horse imported in to England would have been called a 'Turk'.

Second on Blundeville's list was the 'Horse

THE THOROUGHBRED WAS BRED TO MEET THE DEMANDS OF ROYALTY AND THE NOBILITY FOR RACING PURPOSES.

of Barbary', the modern Barb, described as 'little horses but very swift and able to make a long cariere [gallop]'. Blundeville goes on to list horses from Sardinia, Naples, and Corsica, the Spanish 'Jenett', the 'Highe Alamagne' (Hungarian), and the 'Iryshe Hobbye'.

By this time in England, horse racing had become extremely popular and the horses raced were variously described as 'Galloways', 'Running Horses' and 'Hobbies'. Henry VIII established a royal stud at Hampton Court with others at Malmesbury and Tetbury, while James I later imported numerous oriental stallions, including the Markham Arabian, bought in Constantinople, which is reputed to have finished last in every race it ran.

Later monarchs maintained a strong interest in race horse studs: Charles II was supplied with a number of horses and mares each year, many of which he presented to his favorites at court. On Charles's death, numerous stallions but only one brood mare remained in the Royal Stable. This was the period of the famous 'tap-root' mares: 30 mares housed in Yorkshire, from which every living Thoroughbred is descended.

Of the Thoroughbred's original ancestors, three stallions are the most important because from them, all modern Thoroughbreds descend in the male line. The first stallion, the Byerley Turk, which possibly had Turkmene blood, had been captured at the Siege of Vienna and was later used as a charger by a Captain Byerley at the Battle of the Boyne in 1690 before standing at stud.

The second stallion was the Darley Arabian, bought in Aleppo, Syria in 1704, certified as pure-bred and sent to the Darley estates in East Yorkshire. The third stallion was the Godolphin Barb (or Arabian) which was bought in Paris in 1730. The ancestry of this stallion which was at stud in Cambridgeshire, is uncertain and hotly disputed to this day.

Around this time British Thoroughbred horses began to be exported: in 1730, Bulle Rocke, a son of the Darley Arabian was exported to America. After 1770, Arabs ceased to be used in breeding in Britain since improved results were being achieved with homebred stock. Today, Thoroughbred breeding in the U.K. takes place in the racing centers around Newmarket in Suffolk, Lambourne in Berkshire, and Malton in Yorkshire.

Chapter 2
Modern Horse
Classification

The equine world today is divided into a number of classifications. The three main classifications are: Heavy Horse, Light Horse and Pony.

Heavy Horses

Heavy Horses are the 'agricultural' breeds, which until quite recently were part of everyday life on farms and in towns across Europe. Descended from the medieval destrier or warhorse, these are the 'gentle giants' of the horse world, standing up to 18.2 hh, and were used before the advent of steam engines or the internal combustion engine, as draft horses. Today, their role is most often ceremonial, especially as regimental drum horses, although many brewery companies continue to keep and work dray teams.

THE HEAVY CLYDESDALE DRUM HORSES.

Light Horses

The term 'Light Horse' defines those horses used as carriage horses or 'under the saddle'. Light horses stand between 15 and 17.2 hh, with a narrow frame and long legs, and are fast and agile, with some

MANY LIGHT HORSES WERE USED AS CAVALRY MOUNTS, OR, LIKE THIS LIPIZZANER, WERE TRAINED IN ELEGANT 'CLASSICAL' RIDING.

LIGHT HORSES WERE OFTEN USED FOR MILITARY PURPOSES.

breeds particularly noted for their stamina, such as the Akhal-Teke. For centuries, light horses have been used as transport and in the military as cavalry mounts, but alongside these, 'classical' riding was also developed as an art form, which is most evident in the magnificent Lipizzaner horses of the Spanish Riding School in Vienna.

Ponies

The word 'pony' comes from the 17th century French word *poulenet*, meaning 'foal'. Ponies share a common ancestry with horses, but are different from them in several ways: they stand below 15 hh, and have different proportions. In relation to their height, ponies have short legs: their body height at the withers is shorter than the length of their body, while the length of their shoulders is the same as that of their head. Ponies also tend to have longer manes and tails than horses, and shaggier coats. They also have a different 'action', being more sure-footed on harder, smaller feet. Most pony riders will also attest to the fact that ponies can also be very spirited – some displaying an 'instinctive' cunning'.

A further distinction is made between horses that are 'hot bloods', 'warmbloods' and 'cold bloods'. Because of the ancestry from the Forest horses of the cold regions of northern Europe, Heavy horses are also

ALTHOUGH SHARING A COMMON ANCESTRY WITH HORSES, PONIES HAVE SEVERAL DIFFERENCES.

classified as 'cold bloods'. Arabs, and Barbs, along with their direct derivative, the Thoroughbred, are termed 'hot bloods', a term which refers to the unique purity of line that is not shared with any other horses in the world. 'Warmblood' refers to horses combining both hot and cold blood in various proportions.

Horse Breeds

The term 'breed' refers to horses registered in a stud book. These horses have been selectively bred over a long period of time in order to ensure a continuous and consistent production of horses sharing common and defined characteristics regarding size, conformation (the shape and proportions of a horse's body), action (the movement of the legs at all paces) and sometimes, color.

Horse types

There are, in addition to horse breeds, the horse types. Types are those horses which do not qualify for breed status because they do have a fixed character or conformation. Nevertheless, despite an unknown pedigree, these horses do have a distinctive 'look', and the types include cobs, hacks, hunters, and polo ponies.

A cob (except for the Welsh Cob which is a distinct breed) is any horse between 14 and 15 hh that is stocky and strongly built: according to an old adage, the ideal cob is said to have 'a head like a lady's maid and a farewell (backside) like a cook'. In character, a cob is described as 'confidential', that is, safe and dependable, or more endearingly, as 'a gentleman's gentleman'.

THERE ARE A NUMBER OF 'TYPES' OF HORSE WHICH DO NOT QUALIFY FOR BREED STATUS, BUT WHICH NONETHELESS HAVE DISTINCTIVE CHARACTERISTICS, SUCH AS THE COB.

The hack, or show hack as it is known in Britain, derives its name (like the Hackney horse, page 167) from the French Norman word *haquenée*, which was in use in England for many centuries to describe a light horse for general riding purposes, as distinct from the mighty war-horse. In the 19th century, there were two types of hack: the 'covert hack', which was the horse that an owner rode out to the hunt meet before changing to the first of his two hunters assigned to carry him behind the hounds, and the 'park hack', a far more elegant horse, on which the fashionably dressed rider might display himself – and take a little exercise at the same time – in elegant surroundings, such as London's Rotten Row, in Hyde Park. When motor cars became the transport of choice, hacks fell out of use and became largely confined to the show ring, where its elegance and action, are best displayed. There are three classes of hack: the small hack (14.2-15 hh) and the large hack (with an upper limit of 15.3 hh) and the ladies' hack, (between 14.2-15.33 hh which are shown under side saddle). In Europe, hacks are often bred out of pony mares from a Thoroughbred sire or part-bred Arabs or Anglo-Arabs, while in America, the Saddlebred is favored (see

THE HACK WAS ORIGINALLY THE RIDING HORSE OF CHOICE IN BRITAIN.

page 126). This is an American breed which evolved during the 19th century in the southern states, particularly around Kentucky and preserved the gaits of two 'pacing' horses, the Canadian Pacer and the Narragansett Pacer.

Hunters, as their name suggests, are horses used for hunting and are British and Irish in origin because these countries were the birthplace of European fox hunting. Hunters are now to be found in every country where riding to hounds takes place. The type of horse preferred varies from country to country and the type of terrain

**THE HUNTER IS USED ANYWHERE IN THE WORLD
WHERE RIDING TO HOUNDS IS DONE.**

which is crossed. Hunter sires are generally
Thoroughbred: the greater the amount of
Thoroughbred blood, the greater the speed
of the Hunter. Irish Hunters are based on
Thoroughbred-Irish Draft cross, while other
possible crosses are with Cleveland Bay,
Shire, and Clydesdale, the offspring of
which retain the strength and stamina of the
Heavy Horses coupled with the speed of the
Thoroughbred.

Polo Ponies

One of the world's oldest games, polo
originated in Persia some 2,500 years ago.
In Persian, the game was called *changar*,
meaning 'mallet' but the word 'polo' itself
comes from the Tibetan word for ball, *pulu*.
The game was discovered in the 19th
century by British officers serving in the
North-West Frontier in India.

In 1859, a European polo club was
founded in the Caher Valley of Manipur,
India, where the ponies were no more than
49 in. (12.2 hh). The game was introduced
to England in 1869 and was first played at
the home of the British Army at Aldershot,
where it was nicknamed 'hockey on

horseback'. Soon however, polo became
part of the fashionable London 'season'
and became centered at Hurlingham Club,
in west London, which formulated the rules
and became the headquarters of the game.

The game soon spread across the world,
and at first native ponies were used:
Chinese ponies played in Hong Kong and
Shanghai; Arabs in Egypt and the Sudan,
and in the Argentine, and on the cattle
ranches of the western states of America,
the cow pony was used. The ideal polo type
was, however, the American or English
Thoroughbred, the result of crossing a
'dwarf' Thoroughbred measuring 14.2 hh
with native pony mares. In Argentina, the
Thoroughbred was crossed with the native
Criollo, one of the toughest breeds in the
world. The height limit of 14.2 hh was set
in 1899, but was abolished in 1916 when
the height increased to a maximum 15.3
hh. Consequently, the modern polo pony is
actually a small horse.

Chapter 3
Anatomy, Movement, and Appearance

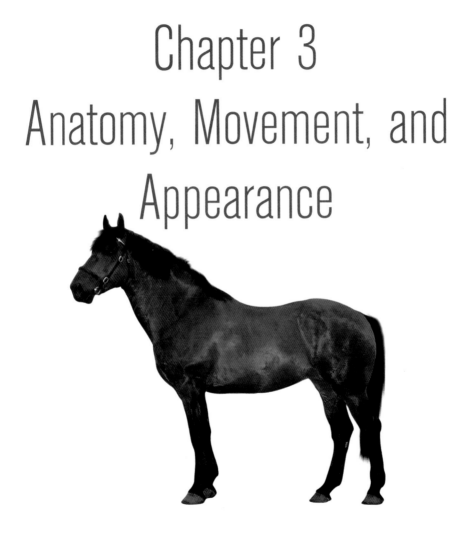

With large teeth for grinding vegetation, large eyes, and good hearing making it alert to danger, and strong legs with feet specially designed for speed in flight, the horse is well adapted to grazing and running. The shape and characteristics of a horse are called its conformation. This is largely the result of the shape of the skeleton and its overlying tissues, and in the proportions and relationship of one part with another. In the U.K. and the U.S.A., horses are measured in hands, expressed as 'hands high' (hh). A hand is 14 in., while in Europe horses are measured in centimeters.

Points of the Horse

The external features which make up a horse's conformation are called the points and no one point or feature should be out of proportion with any of the others.

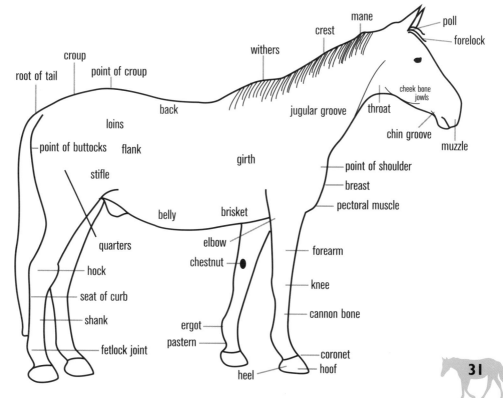

mane
crest
poll
forelock
withers
croup
point of croup
root of tail
cheek bone
jowls
back
jugular groove
throat
loins
chin groove
point of buttocks   flank
muzzle
girth
stifle
point of shoulder
breast
belly   brisket
pectoral muscle
quarters
elbow
forearm
chestnut
hock
knee
seat of curb
cannon bone
shank
ergot
pastern
fetlock joint
coronet
hoof
heel

SKELETON OF HORSE AT HARAS NATIONAL, BLOIS.

Proportions

There are three significant proportions. The first is the measurement from the top of the withers to the deepest part of the body behind and below the elbow. This should equal the distance from that point to the ground and is to allow for the unrestricted expansion of the lungs.

The second measurement regards the length of the neck. In the interests of balance – and where speed is a requirement – the neck should be 1⅓ times the measurement taken from the poll down the front of the face, to the lower lip.

The third measurement is from the point of the shoulder to the last of the asternal ribs (false ribs). This must be twice the length from the rear of the wither to the highest part of the croup. If the proportions (the conformation) of a horse are good, not only will the horse perform or work better, but they will also be more 'attractive'.

Gaits

The horse's skeleton is held together firmly by tough, flexible ligaments which allow for free movement and work to prevent over-extension of the joints which can result in injury and damage. The structure is covered by muscles which produce the movement in the limbs by contracting and extending. Lack of muscle development, or incorrect training will result in a horse whose carriage and movement is 'faulty' and inefficient.

The way a horse's legs are used is called the action. This varies between breeds and types: heavy horses, with their straighter shoulders, bend their knees giving them greater traction and pulling power. Light horses bend their knees less and the result is a long, smooth stride, while a pony's 'springy ride' is the result of their picking their feet high in action.

Four paces are used by horses as a whole: the walk, trot, canter, and gallop. In each of these paces the horse's hooves touch the ground in a different sequence, and these sequences are called gaits.

DIAGONALS IN TROTTING.

The Walk

At a speed of about 3 miles per hour, the walk is a four-beat pace during which the horse places its feet on the ground in equal-length strides, with each lateral pair of feet placed on the ground together. The sequence of footfalls is: near (left) hind, near fore, off (right) hind, off fore. In modern dressage, four sub-divisions of the walk are required: the medium, collected, extended and free.

The Trot

This is a two-beat pace during which the horse places a diagonal pair of feet on the ground together, then springs up, and then places the other diagonal pair down with just a moment of suspension between each step, when all four feet are off the ground. The sequence is: near hind and off forelegs down together, then off hind and near forelegs together. In modern dressage there are four sub-divisions of the trot: collected, working, medium and extended.

AT ONE POINT IN MID-CANTER, ALL FOUR LEGS WILL BE OFF THE GROUND.

The Canter

The canter is a three-beat pace followed by a moment of suspension when all the hooves are off the ground at the same time. When circling, the sequence of the legs are: off hind leg, followed by right diagonal pair (off fore and near hind together), followed by near foreleg, off hind together (left diagonal together), then off fore (the leading leg). Experienced riders are able to make their horses change the leading leg in mid-canter, and this is known as a 'flying change'.

THE ICELANDIC HORSE HAS AN EXTRA, FIFTH GAIT.

The Gallop

The fastest of the natural gaits, the top speed of a gallop is about 43 mph, but this high speed cannot be maintained for very long. The gallop is generally a four-beat gait, but there can be variations depending on the speed. The sequence is: near hind leg, then off hind leg, then near fore leg, then off fore leg, then all four feet are off the ground together before the near hind leg touches down again.

These sequences were for many years in dispute and were only 'proved' by Eadweard Muybridge's (1830-1907) photographic experiments of animal locomotion in the 1870s. In addition to the four natural gaits, there are also some specialized ones including ambling and pacing which are used in harness racing. The Icelandic horse has five gaits – the walk, trot, gallop, the *skeið* or pace, and a unique, four-beat running walk called the *tölt* which is used to cross difficult terrain.

Coat Colors

The various coat colors of the world's horses are governed by genetics. It was the Austrian monk, Gregor Mendel (1822-84) who devised the laws that governed hereditary characteristics which formed the basis of modern genetic science. Each cell in a horse's body contains two genes, one from each parent. One of these genes is dominant, the other is recessive: it is the dominant gene in the pair which will prevail in the offspring. Understanding genetics allows breeders to predict the coat color of an unborn foal. In horses, gray is the coat color which is dominant over all others.

AMERICAN CRÈME DRAFT COAT COLOR.

AFTER GRAY, BAY IS THE COLOR WHICH IS MOST DOMINANT.

GRAY IS THE MOST DOMINANT COAT COLOR.

DARK BROWN TRAKEHNER.

DARK BAY BASHKIR STALLION.

Gray refers to a black skin with a mixture of black and white hairs. There are also flea-bitten, and dapple-gray coats. The first has brown specks of hair flecking an otherwise gray coat, while the second has dark gray hairs forming rings on a gray base.

The order of dominance for other colors is: bay (reddish-brown coat with a black mane, tail and points); brown (mixed black and brown hairs with a black mane, tail and legs); black (black hair, sometimes with white marks), and, chestnut (various shades of gold from pale to red-gold. Liver-chestnut is the appellation for the very darkest of this shade).

Bay is dominant over the other colors which follow it, and chestnut is always recessive. Consequently, two chestnut horses will produce a chestnut foal, but a chestnut crossed with another color are less likely to do so. Other 'solid colors' are dun (black skin with yellowish hair), roan (black skin with a solid coat mixed with white) Variations on roan include strawberry-roan (a chestnut coat with white hairs) and blue-roan (a black or brown body with white hairs).

A BLUE ROAN SHETLAND MARE.

In some breeds, color is important, although conformation and health are considered more important. The Palomino coloring is a black or brown muzzle, a golden coat, flaxen mane and tail with no white markings on the body, although they are permitted on the legs.

Spotted horses like the Colorado Ranger or the Appaloosa, are known as 'part-colored' or 'colored breeds'. Their coloring is the legacy of the early Spanish horses taken by the conquistadors to the New World in the 16th century. There are five patterns of spotted horses:

blanket, marble, leopard, snowflake, and frost (white speckling on a dark background). The skin of spotted horses is a mottled pink.

Piebald means large patches of black and white. There are two forms of piebald: overo, a solid color base with white patches, and tobiano, a white coat with solid patches of color. Skewbald refers to a coat with large patches of white and any color except black. Confusingly, the Americans often use the term 'Pinto' (paint) to mean either a piebald or skewbald horse.

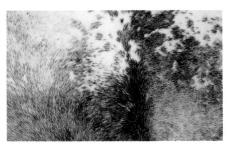

APPALOOSA, BLANKET PATTERN.

A TENNESSEE WALKING HORSE, SPOTTED, TOBIANO

PAINT, THE U.S. TERM FOR PIEBALD OR SKEWBALD.

Markings

There are two types of markings on horses: natural marks and man-made marks such as brands (either from hot irons or by freezing) which stop the hair on the design from growing back and create a permanent mark used to identify the ownership of a horse and prevent theft. Natural marks are areas of different color from that of the background. These can be very distinctive and in pedigree horses are carefully documented. Natural marks which occur on the face of a horse are designated star (a white spot on the forehead), stripe, blaze (a white area down the center of the face), white face, white muzzle, or mealy muzzle, and snip. On the legs, the markings are called stockings when they are white, up to and over the knee; socks when they are white up to the knee; and ermine when they are black spots on white markings around the coronet.

Markings on the body include zebra stripes – rings of dark hair on the legs; a dorsal stripe – almost always found with a dun coat, and flesh mottling, which is generally found on part-colored horses' coats. The hooves, too, may have markings: blue hoof is a hoof of slate blue-colored horn; white hoof is white horn and is usually to be found on horses with white socks or stockings, while striped hooves can be found on horses with spotted coats.

Docked Tails and Hogged Manes

Two terms are used to describe a horse's mane or tail: docking and hogging (known as roaching in the U.S.A.). Docking refers to the permanent amputation of the tail for aesthetic reasons alone. In 1948, the Docking and Nicking Act made this illegal in the U.K. 'Nicking' is the division and resetting of the muscles under the tail to give an artificially high carriage. A hogged mane is a mane that has been (temporarily) removed by clipping it close to the neck. Polo ponies, as well as Cobs, are hogged today to show off their thick, muscular necks, but their tails are, thankfully, left full.

Chapter 4
Wild Horses, Asses, Hemionids, and Zebras

Around one million years ago, the horse family split into two branches. One branch led to zebras, donkeys, hemionids (wild asses,) and mules. The second branch led, via the Tarpan, the Forest Horse and the Asiatic Wild Horse (also known as Przewalski's Horse) to the modern horse.

Zebras

These beautifully striped animals are to be found distributed throughout southern Africa. At one time there were many species but today only three species and seven subspecies survive. The three species differ from each other both in the striping of their coats and in other physical respects.

The largest zebra, standing at around 13.2 hh (53 inches) and weighing around 950 lb is Grevy's Zebra, which can be found in the far north of the region, although it is now a rare animal with only some 7,000 still in existence. Grevy's Zebras are identified by their numerous narrow body stripes and a white belly. This was the first animal to split away from the first single-hoofed horse, Pliohippus. The Grevy's Zebra is classified in the subgenus

Dolichohippus, while the other two species, the Cape Mountain Zebra (*Equus [hippotigris] zebra*) which is also endangered, and Burchell's Zebra (*Equus [hippotigris] burchelli*), the zebra most commonly found in zoos are more closely related to horses and asses and are classified in the subgenus of Hippotigris.

The most abundant of the zebras is the Plains, or Common Zebra, which roam the grasslands of eastern Africa in large herds. Of the seven recognized subspecies which differ from one another by stripe patterns, the most widespread is Grant's Zebra with its broad sweeping flank stripes, and which accounts for nearly 70% of the Common Zebra population.

Zebra Hybrids

The term 'zebra hybrid' is an all-embracing term for a zebra crossed with any other equine. The term Zorse is used to describe the cross of a zebra stallion to a horse mare. Other terms that are often seen are Zeborid, Zony (a zebra-pony cross) or Zeony. Zebra-donkey crosses are termed Zebroid, Zebrass, Zonkey or Ze-donk.

Hybrids are always interesting curiosities: the mule is perhaps the most well known hybrid, the combination of a horse and a donkey. But hybrids are not easy to create because the mating pairs have different number of chromosomes (the 'packets' of DNA in each cell) and successful pregnancies are rare. A horse has 64 chromosomes: the zebra has only 44. The rare, resulting zorse from a successful cross breed will have a number of chromosomes that are somewhere in between the two. A zorse can only result when the sire is a zebra: the smaller number of chromosomes must be on the male side. If it was the other way round, there would be no pregnancy. Furthermore, the progeny of such zebra-horse crosses are invariably sterile.

While zebras appear to have 'ponyish' bodies, they have different hip shapes. Their ears are also larger and rounder than those of horses: the Cape Mountain Zebra's ears are almost donkey-like, while the Grevy's Zebra ears are a huge conical shape. The necks, likewise, are characteristically straight in 'long ears' and most donkeys and zebras lack true withers (so saddles are difficult to fit). Their manes are stiff and upright and both zebras and donkeys lack forelocks. Zebras have a variety of noises, the most common of which is 'barking' or the 'qua-ha' sound:

all these traits are passed along in part to zebra hybrid offspring.

Of the many variations in the striping patterns in the zebra, three are most commonly seen in zebra hybrid breeding: the flank stripes of the Grant Zebra, the 'shadow stripes' of the Damarland Zebra, and the narrow stripes and white belly of the Grevy Zebra. However, no matter what the exact patterning of the zebra sire, many 'zebroids' will have more stripes over their hips and backs than their parent. Typically 'zebroids' will have boldly striped legs, a clearly visible dorsal eel stripe, and varying degrees of striping on the face, neck, shoulders and body. The stripes may be dark brown or black against coats of all horse colors, or may even appear as red on chestnut or sorrel coats.

Depending on the parents, zebroids will be either more 'horse-like' or more 'ass-like' in body, and they are usually smaller than most horses or mules. The Zorse is in general much stronger and much hardier than the horse: from the zebra comes not only the stripes but natural athleticism – making the Zorse a natural jumper. A yearling Zorse foal can easily clear a 6 ft fence with great speed, so perhaps one day there will be 'Race Zorses'!

Hemionids

In zoological terms hemionid means 'half-ass', a rather unfortunate term because it suggests an animal that is half-ass, half-something else. It is actually used to describe an animal that has the nature and some of the characteristics of both a horse and an ass, although it will probably also have many distinctive features of its own, such as the length of the lower leg bones, which in hemionids are much longer than in any other form of Equus.

There are two groups of ass, the Asiatic and the African. The Asiatic ass has been domesticated for around 6,000 years, with herds being kept by the ancient Egyptians. The Asiatic Ass, or now extinct Onager, is the 'wild ass' of the Bible but there are many subspecies living today throughout Asia and the Middle East, including the Mongolian Khulan (*Equus hemionus hemionus*) or Jigetai as it is called locally in the desert areas of central Asia; the Tibetan Kiang, and, the Indian Ghorkar, now endangered and fighting for survival in the Rann of Kutch in northern India.

The African Wild Ass (*Equus asinus*) is the ancestor of the domestic donkey and was described to the scientific community by Linnaeus in 1758. It is mostly found in hilly and stony desert, the arid to semi-arid bush lands and grasslands in the northeast of Africa. At one time it was probably widespread from the Atlas Mountains in Morocco across Saharan and Sahelian Africa to Sudan and Somalia, and possibly extending into the Arabian Peninsula. Because it feeds on grasses, access to water is essential – although the wild ass can survive for much longer than any other equid, it needs water every second or third day. In the 1960s the African Wild Ass could be found in Ethiopia and in Somalia, and in the 1970s in the Sudan until severe drought devastated the land. It is now thought that only small and endangered populations may still be found in the coastal regions of the Red Sea in Djibouti, Eritrea, Somalia, Ethiopia and possibly, Sudan.

In addition to drought, interbreeding between wild and domestic animals contributed to the decline of the African Wild Ass population, which was further damaged by the introduction of firearms used for hunting the wild ass for food and to kill off animals which herders believed was consuming the valuable vegetation reserved for their domestic livestock. Civil unrest and war in the region also contributed to the decline, but it is also reported that many specimens died of exhaustion after being chased by tourists' vehicles as they tried to photograph the now rare animal.

One of the subspecies of the African Wild Ass is the Somali Wild Ass (*E. a. somalicus* from Somalia and Ethiopia): this is one of the most endangered species and there are estimated to be only about 200 in the wild and only about 80 in zoos world wide. In the United Kingdom, Marwell Zoological Park is the only one to have this rare and beautiful animal and where recently three foals were born: Hartley (born July 23, 2002), Hector (born July 30,

SOMALI WILD ASS

2002) and Florrie (born August 5, 2002). The Somali Wild Ass have a subtle blue-gray body color, a pale under body and pale legs with distinctive horizontal black stripes resembling those of a zebra. They also have the dorsal eel stripe and the stiff upright mane, the hairs of which are tipped with black. The ears are large with black margins and the tail terminates with a black brush. The hooves are slender and about the same diameter as the legs.

Swift and sure-footed in their rough, rocky habitat, the African Wild Asses have been clocked at speeds up to 30 mph and are active in the cooler hours of late afternoon and early morning, seeking shade and shelter among the rocks during the heat of the day.

Donkeys

The domestic ass, or donkeys, (*Equus asinus*) are descended from the African Wild asses and for the most part, have the 'primitive' markings associated with the dun factor in horses.

Dun as a coat color is actually a dilution that works on the color of the body, but does not affect the extremities such as the head, lower legs, mane and tail.

The name donkey was not in common use until the 18th century and appears to have come from the combination of 'dun', referring to the coat color, and 'kin' meaning 'small'.

Male donkeys are called 'jacks', females are called 'jennets' and the average height of the common donkey is around 40 in. at the withers. There are, however, dwarf donkeys such as those found on the Italian island of Sicily, and in India, which can be as small as 24 in., while the Andalusian jack donkey from Spain can reach 15 hh (60 inches). Donkeys may be black, gray, white and even part-colored but they all

have the dorsal eel stripe running down the back and the 'shoulder cross' at right angles over it at the withers, making up the cross-shaped mark said to have been placed on them in memory of the donkey that carried Jesus into Jerusalem prior to his Crucifixion.

Unlike horses, donkeys do not have chestnuts on their hind legs and they have five lumbar vertebrae rather than a horse's six. They also have the short upright mane and long ears that are testament to their Wild Ass ancestry – as well as the characteristic bray which is quite unlike the neigh of a horse. One of the largest, and the most famous donkeys, is the Baudet de Poitou, or the Poitevin jackass, from the Poitou region of France. This is a huge animal that is very carefully bred for size and conformation and is used to sire the Poitevin mules from heavy Mulassier (Poitevin) mares.

Asiatic Wild Horse

While the wild asses, zebras, donkeys, and mules, form one branch of the equid tree, the second branch, which leads to the modern horse, was by way of the Tarpan and the Asiatic Wild Horse (*Equus caballus przewalskii przewalski Poliakov*). Also called Przewalski's Horse, it is the only one of the primitive founders of the modern equine races to survive in its original form. In prehistoric times, the Asiatic Wild Horse lived on the European and Central Asian Steppes east of longitude 40 degrees.

PRZEWALSKI'S HORSE

TARPAN

Today, the Asiatic Wild Horse is preserved in a number of zoos, but selected groups have been returned to the wild.

Once though to be extinct, wild herds of this Mongolian horse were discovered by Colonel Nikolai Mikhailovitch Przewalski of the Russian Imperial Army in 1879 in the area of Tachin Schah (the Mountains of the Yellow Horse) on the edge of the Gobi Desert. Przewalski was given the skin of one of these 'yellow horses' by local Kyrghyz hunters, who knew the horse as the 'Taki'. From 1899 expeditions were sent to capture specimens so they could be studied in scientific detail. It was soon realized that the Asiatic Wild Horse was a unique animal.

The Asiatic Wild Horse differs from its domestic descendants in the number of chromosomes: it has 66 rather than the 64 of the domestic horse. It is also aggressive and fierce and is said to be migratory, moving north in winter and returning south in the spring. The Asiatic Wild Horse stands on average 13 hh (52 in.) and is a sand-dun color with black legs — which are often striped like those of a zebra — and has a black mane and tail. There is usually a

pronounced dorsal stripe, sometimes with an accompanying cross over the shoulder (see donkeys above) while the mane displays the prominent 'primitive' feature: it stands upright and grows to a length of about 8 inches without 'falling over' the neck like a horse's mane would when this is allowed to grow long. The mane is of an especially harsh texture and on the upper part of the tail, the hairs are short, like those of a donkey or mule.

Like the zebra and the khulan (with which it is often confused), the Asiatic Wild Horse is straight-backed and has no discernible withers. While the Asiatic Wild Horse resembles the asinine group, it is a member of *Equus caballus*, and the last truly wild type of horse or pony on which no attempts at domestication have been made. The similarities between the Asiatic Wild Horse and the members of the 'other branch' of the equid tree, simply show how close they both are to a common root.

Chapter 5
Horse Breeds

Ponies

Sometime around 6,000 years ago – just before the first horses were being domesticated – it is believed that two separate types of ponies evolved on the plains and steppes of central Eurasia. Pony Type 1 is most likely descended from Tarpan stock, and continued to develop in north–west Europe. Pony Type 2 is probably descended from the Asiatic Wild Horse (*Equus caballus przewalskii przewalski Poliakov*) and developed in northern Eurasia.

These ponies developed long before the end of the Ice Age, when Britain was still attached by an ice bridge to continental Europe. When the last bridge disappeared around 15,000 BC, the horses and ponies already in Britain were effectively cut off from any further equine influences. It would not be until the Bronze Age, around 1,000 BC when ships were being built that were strong enough to carry livestock and horses, that other types of horses were seen in Britain. Consequently, the ponies 'stranded' at the end of the Ice Age had some 14,000 years to develop their fixed characters. When invaders and traders such as the Romans, Vikings and the Phoenicians, arrived, they brought with them new horses whose genes would influence and mingle with some of the British pony breeds.

Britain has a number of native pony breeds, often referred to as Moorland or Mountain breeds because of their original habitats. Today there are no truly feral stocks of ponies in Britain: the most 'wild' herds such as the Exmoor ponies are rounded up annually for breed and veterinary inspection, although many owners still keep the ponies in their 'original' environments. These breeds have been 'improved' over the centuries, but nevertheless continue to retain special qualities and characteristics that are the result of particular environmental conditions and their long period of geographical isolation. Breed societies today maintain stud books to ensure that all stock is pure–bred. Another British breed is the Lundy Pony (see page 78) which was established in 1928.

Across mainland Europe and Scandinavia, there are ponies of equally ancient origin. Today many of these ponies are working animals, employed on farms in the rural economies of central and eastern Europe.

In the more industrialised and wealthy western European nations, increasing numbers of ponies of riding quality are being bred to for recreation and leisure pursuits. In North, South, and Central America, ponies arrived with the Spanish Conquistadors and were developed later into a wide variety of pony breeds including the tiny Falabella (see page 63), and the Chincoteague (see page 53). Meanwhile, in Asia, the world's largest continent extending from the Arctic Circle in the north to the Equator in the south, there are numerous pony breeds which have developed according to the widely varied climates and terrain of the continent.

Bashkir Pony

The Bashkir, or Bashkirsky, takes its name from Bashkiria, in the southern foothills of the Ural Mountains, close to the steppes of Kirghizia and Kazakhstan. Like most ponies, the Bashkir is naturally hardy, but in its native lands, theses ponies live out all year round – often in deep snow and in temperatures of 30°–40° C below freezing (-22° to -40° F) subsisting on the most frugal of diets.

In spite of these conditions the Bashkir mares are famous for their milk production: in a seven- to eight-month lactation period, an average mare will give upwards of 1,500 litres (330 gallons) of milk. Much of this is used in dairy produce but some is reserved for making Kummis, the 'fire water' of the steppes! Like many horses and ponies, the Bashkir also provided its owners with another valuable source of protein in the form of its meat. The Bashkir also gives freely of its thick, curly coat and its luxurious mane and tail: combings from the pony's hair can be woven to make blankets and clothing.

Height: **13–14 hh. (1.32–1.42 m)**
Colors: **Chestnut, dun, bay**
Use: **Saddle, Pack, Draft, Milk and Meat**
Features: **Thick curly coat, luxurious mane and tail, hard feet (usually unshod), heavy head on thick, strong neck.**

Additionally, the Bashkir can be used under saddle, as a mountain pack pony, and in draft, their endurance is legendary: it is said that a Bashkir troika (a sledge pulled by three horses abreast) can easily cover 120–140 km (75–85 miles) per day through the snow.

contribution of the Bashkir to the local economies of the southern Urals, breeding centers were established in 1845 to improve stock, and two types of pony have been developed: the mountain type, suitable for riding, and the heavier steppe variety.

In America, Bashkir type ponies, called Bashkir Curlies, are found in the northwestern states, where it is said they were first seen in Mustang herds (page 228) in the early 19th century. Some maintain that the Bashkir arrived in America thousands of years ago, via the Bering Strait. This is unlikely, since the horse in the Americas became extinct some 8,000–10,000 years ago and was not reintroduced there until the 16th century by the Spanish.

Caspian Pony

Height: **10–12 hh. (40-48 in.)**
Colors: **Bay, chestnut, gray, brown**
Use: **Saddle, harness**
Features: **Large, gazelle-like eyes, very short ears (breed standard stipulates no longer than 4 ½ inches. Full flowing mane and tail which is carried high. Strong, small feet which are very rarely shod. Natural jumping ability.**

The Caspian pony, a native of the area around the Elburtz Mountains and Caspian Sea in Iran, is one of the world's most ancient horse breeds and represents a link between the early forms of *Equus* and the hot blooded or 'plateau' horses from which the modern light horses have evolved. Just prior to the domestication of the horse, there were four subspecies in existence: the two pony types and the two horse types. The last of these, Horse Type 4, was the smallest, standing no more than 9 hh, but with regard to its proportions, it was a horse. Its native habitat was western Asia, and it is suggested that Horse Type 4 was the prototype of the Arab (see pages 113–121).

'Miniature' horses of decidedly Arab appearance appear on many examples of art from ancient Egypt and Mesopotamia, and around 500 BC, similar horses were depicted on the seal of the Persian king, Darius the Great (522-486 BC). This seal shows a pair of these horses drawing a chariot from which Darius shoots arrows at an attacking lion – a lion so huge it dwarfs the horses. Miniature horses were also recorded in existence by the ancient Greeks in parts of Medea, the area south of the Caspian Sea, while horse remains have been found in caves from the Mesolithic period in Kermansh (an area midway between Baghdad in Iraq, and Tehran in Iran). It appears that around 1,000 years ago the tribes from Kermansh moved from the region, and, along with their horses, settled on the northern edge of the Elburtz Mountains.

The Caspian pony is distinguished from other breeds by several unique physical characteristics: there is a marked difference in the shape of the scapula (more like that of a horse than a pony), there is an extra molar in the upper jaw, and, a different formation of the parietal bones of the head which give a 'vaulted' appearance to the skull. Thought to be extinct, these ponies were 'rediscovered' pulling carts in Amol, in northern Iran in 1965 by American traveller, Mrs Louise I. Firouz. Subsequently, a selective breeding program was established to safeguard the Caspian's future and there are now studs in Iran, and Caspian societies in Britain, the U.S.A., Australia, and New Zealand.

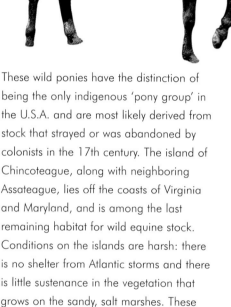

Chincoteague Pony

Height: average 12 hh. (48 in.)
Colors: Any, many are paint or pinto (piebald and skewbald)
Use: Mainly feral, but some under saddle
Features: Short round body, shaggy winter coat, many are light boned with poorly developed joints

These wild ponies have the distinction of being the only indigenous 'pony group' in the U.S.A. and are most likely derived from stock that strayed or was abandoned by colonists in the 17th century. The island of Chincoteague, along with neighboring Assateague, lies off the coasts of Virginia and Maryland, and is among the last remaining habitat for wild equine stock. Conditions on the islands are harsh: there is no shelter from Atlantic storms and there is little sustenance in the vegetation that grows on the sandy, salt marshes. These conditions meant that only the toughest, hardiest and most adaptable ponies survived. These harsh conditions took their toll and by the early 20th century, much of the stock was showing signs of stunted growth, and more serious conformation distortions associated with uncontrolled inbreeding in an isolated and restricted gene pool.

Around 200 Chincoteague ponies (pronounced shin-ca-teeg), live on the larger Assateague Island and in the 1920s, knowledge of this feral breed became more widespread when the Chincoteague Volunteer Fire Department assumed responsibility for the ponies and improved the stock by introducing Shetland (see page 76), Welsh Pony, and Pinto (see page 205) blood. The Pinto out-crosses have produced part-colored ponies as well as a more 'horsey' appearance to the Chincoteague's head.

Connemara Pony

Height: 13–14.2 hh. (52–57 in.)
Colors: Bay, gray, black, dun, brown
Use: Saddle, harness
Features: Small head on graceful neck, strong legs, sure-footed, natural jumpers. Suitable for child and adult riders.

Ireland's only indigenous pony, the Connemara takes its name from the county in the west of Ireland. The region faces the Atlantic Ocean and is famed for its magnificent landscape of lakes, moors, bog lands, and mountains. The Connemara's ancestors were likely to have been ponies that were similar to the Shetland (see page 76) and Norwegian Fjord (see page 75) but when Celtic raiders arrived in the 5th and 6th centuries, an eastern influence was introduced by the small Celtic pony. Later, when Galway became an important trading center in the 16th century, Spanish horses were brought in, and it is also said that Spanish blood was introduced from horses saved from the wrecks of the Spanish Armada in 1588.

In the 19th century 'Arab' blood – though more likely to have been the Barb (see page 21) – was brought to Connemara by wealthy landowners. In 1897, in an attempt to halt the deterioration of the breed, a government-backed scheme introduced Welsh Cobbs (page 84), Thoroughbreds (see page 122), Hackneys (see page 167), and Clydesdales (see page 99). These crosses marked the beginnings of the modern Connemara which is noted as one of the finest performance ponies: fast and courageous, yet sensible, a natural jumper, and extremely versatile, for the Connemara can be ridden

by children and adults alike.

In 1923 the Connemara Pony Breeder Society was established, and in 1926, the stud book was set up. The first stallion to be recorded was Cannon Ball, born in 1906 and still held in awe in the west of Ireland to this day. Cannon Ball won the farmer's Race at Oughterard for 16 years running (locals say he was fed half a barrel of oats the night before the race), and worked in harness his entire life. He was well known for happily trotting home from market with his owner, Harry O'Toole, drunk and snoring on the floor of the cart. Cannon Ball's death was marked with the appropriate Irish traditional ceremonial befitting an admired member of the community: a wake with with plenty of drinking, telling of tales, and singing, that lasted throughout the night – before Cannon Ball was laid to rest in his field at dawn the next morning.

Dales Pony

Height: 14.2 hh. (57 in.)

Colors: Black, dark brown, occasionally gray

Use: Saddle, harness, farm work

Features: Heavy, very deep shoulders; short back and very strong loins, thick mane and tail; short, flat cannons with no less than 8 in. of bone; lower legs are covered in abundant, fine silky feathers.

The Dales pony is one of Britain's heaviest native ponies and hails from the eastern side of the Pennines in the counties of Yorkshire, Northumberland, and County Durham. Genetically, the Dales pony is related to the smaller Fell pony (see page 64) whose traditional breeding area is on the western side of the Pennines.

The Dales pony is probably descended from Friesians (see page 160) brought to Britain by the Romans over 2,000 years ago, and the steep terrain and harsh climate of the region have made them both sure-footed and hardy. In the 18th century, Dales ponies provided the power in the lead mines of Allendale and Alston Moor, working both underground and as pack ponies, carrying lead ore across the rugged landscape of the northeast of England to the seaports on the River Tyne. Later, they were also used in coal mines, largely

because of their ability to bear loads that are out of proportion to their weight: the average weight carried by a Dales pony was 220 lb (2 cwt).

But the Dales pony was also a fine trotter in harness or under saddle and was reputedly able to cover 1 mile in 3 minutes while carrying a considerable load. In order to improve on this, in the 19th century, Welsh Cob (see page 84) blood was introduced – in particular, that of a trotting stallion *par excellence* called Comet. In the early 20th century, crosses were also made with Clydesdales (see page 99) although this was not regarded as a successful move. By 1917 the Dales was considered to be

two-thirds Clydesdale – but was still
regarded as the best pack horse for military
use during World War One. In more recent
times, the influence of the Clydesdale has
diminished, leaving the Dales as a pony
with great stamina, a calm temperament,
and a strong constitution, that is ideally
suited to pony trekking. The trotting quality
is still present however, and, this makes the
Dales pony a particularly fine harness pony
as well.

Dartmoor Pony

Height: **12.2 hh. (49 in.)**

Colors: **Black, bay, brown (only a small amount of white marking is accepted for show and registration purposes.**

Use: **Saddle**

Features: **Noted for its sloping shoulders, small head, alert ears, and the lack of knee lift resulting in a long, low action.**

In Devon, in the southwest of England, lies a vast, windswept area of wild moorland known as Dartmoor, where, for at least 1,000 years, sure-footed and hardy wild ponies have roamed free. From the 12th to the 15th centuries the ponies were used to carry tin from local mines.

The type of pony that lived here has varied through the ages: it was influenced by several different breeds such as the Old Devon Pack Horse and the Cornish Goonhilly (now both extinct), as well as eastern or oriental horses which may have been introduced in the 12th century. In the 19th century, Welsh Ponies and Welsh Cobbs pages 84–85), Arabs page 113) small Thoroughbreds (page 122), and Exmoor Ponies (page 60) were also introduced. In an attempt to produce pit ponies, Shetlands (page 76) were turned out onto the moors: the result was disastrous, with the near disappearance of the tough Dartmoor of good riding type. The breed was saved by the introduction of Welsh Mountain Ponies (see page 85), a Fell Pony (see page 64) and the renowned polo pony stallion, Lord Polo.

In the end, the numerous out-crosses have produced a riding pony with an exceptionally smooth action since the Dartmoor does not lift its knees very high when moving. The ponies were not registered until 1899 when the Dartmoor Section of the Polo Pony Society's (now the National Pony Society) Stud Book was opened and a standard of points drawn up. Interest in the breed gradually rose but during World War Two when Dartmoor was used as a military training area, the breed came close to extinction: only two males and 12 females were registered between 1941 and 1943. Once again, the breed was saved from extinction by a handful of dedicated breeders and today, the majority of Dartmoor ponies are bred on private studs throughout the UK. Sure-footed, kind and sensible, they are ideal riding ponies and are popular in Europe, the U.S.A., and Canada, especially as a child's first pony.

Exmoor Pony

Height: **12–12.3 hh. (48-50 in.)**

Colors: Bay, brown, mousey dun; mealy muzzle and markings around eyes, on underbelly and between thighs. No white markings allowed

Use: Saddle, cross-breeding

Features: Hooded eyes ('toad eyes'); beginnings of a seventh molar tooth; coat almost double–textured; 'ice tail': thick with fanlike growth at top; great powers of endurance.

The Exmoor is Britain's oldest, native breed of pony and retains significant features found in its principal ancestor, Pony Type 1 such as the particular jaw formation with a seventh molar tooth. The Exmoor pony has remained unchanged for centuries, largely because of the isolation of its native high, wild moorlands in northeast Devon, where they have run since the Ice Age. This and the harsh climate of Exmoor has produced a pony that is incredibly strong and exceptionally hardy. On the Rare Breeds Survival Trust's 'critical list', there are now only three principal herds on the moors. The purity and quality of these ponies, which are in a sense 'wild', is carefully safeguarded by the Exmoor Pony Society. Each year in Fall, the herds are rounded up and those foals which pass inspection are branded with a star near the shoulder to indicate that they are pure-bred Exmoors. Beneath the star is the herd number, and on the left hindquarter is the number of the pony in the herd.

Pure-bred Exmoors are instantly recognizable by the mealy-coloured muzzle and markings around the eyes, inside the ears, inside the thighs, and under the belly. No white markings are permitted in the breed standard. The prominent eyes are called 'toad eyes' because they are hooded,

which provides protection against the weather. The Exmoor's head is also a little larger than other breeds because of the length of its nasal passages: the longer length allows for the air to be warmed up before being inhaled into the lungs! The thick tail has a natural fanlike growth at the top: this so-called 'ice tail' protects from snow and rain, as does the coat, which is double textured and waterproof. In winter the coat grows thick, harsh and springy in texture; in summer it is dense and hard with a distinctive metallic sheen. Naturally nervous of humans, Exmoor ponies do make exceptionally good riding ponies when properly trained: enormously strong in proportion to their size, they are also noted for their gallop and their jump. Other Exmoor ponies are bred elsewhere in Britain, but ponies which are bred 'off the moors', away from their natural habitat, tend to loose type.

Eriskay Pony

Height: 12–13.2 hh. (48-53 in.)
Colors: Gray, with occasional black and bay,
Use: Saddle, harness, croft and deer hunt work
Features: Dense, waterproof coat, and thick tail; fine
silky hair on legs.

The harsh and demanding environment of the Western Isles helped to develop a breed of pony over at least 4,000 years that was tough, waterproof, and wind-resistant. Furthermore, on islands where feed was restricted, the Eriskay pony would frequently supplement its meagre diet by feeding off the mineral-rich seaweed on the shoreline.

The ponies of Scotland's Western Isles were crofters' ponies: while the islands' menfolk made their livings from the sea, work on the small farmsteads or crofts, was left largely to the women, children and ponies. The ponies carried peat (the only source of fuel of the islands) and seaweed (used in both dyestuffs and as a fertiliser) in vast creels (baskets) fitted to either side of the pony's back. Strong enough to pull loaded carts over rough ground, the ponies were also hitched to harrows for farm work and acted as school buses for the island's children.

The Eriskay pony is related to the larger Highland pony (see page 69): crossbreeding with the Highland resulted in a reduction in the number of pure-bred ponies left on the island of Eriskay and by 1970 the herd was reduced to around 20 ponies. Fortunately, a number of enthusiasts had sought to re-establish the breed which by then was regarded as the Western Island 'type' of Highland pony. The Eriskay Pony Society has successfully risen the number of ponies to around 300, but the Eriskay is still classified as a threatened rare breed.

Falabella

Height: 7hh. (28 in.)
Colors: All solid and part colors
Use: Pet, not for riding, sometimes shown in harness in the U.S.A.
Features: Miniature horse proportions, luxurious tail and mane, large head in proportion to rest of body.

At various times throughout history miniature horses have been bred as pets and for their 'novelty' value. The Falabella is not really a pony but a miniature horse: it is in fact the smallest horse in the world, and maintains a horse's proportions and character. The very small size of the Falabella makes it completely unsuited to riding, although in the U.S.A. it can sometimes be seen in harness.

The basis of the Falabella was the Shetland pony (see page 76) and possibly, at one time, a very small 'freak' Thoroughbred (see page 122). It was first bred by the Falabella family on their ranch in Argentina by deliberately downsizing with crosses of the smallest animals. In the process, the strength and hardiness of the Shetland has been lost. The smallest Falabella ever bred was Sugar Dumpling, belonging to Smith McCoy of West Virginia, U.S.A., a mere 20 inches high and weighing just 30 lb.

Breeders aim to produce a near-perfect horse in miniature: the preferred height is about 30 in. at the withers. But inbreeding often results in poor conformation: some animals have over large and heavy heads, weak quarters and in some instances, misshapen lower limbs. Nevertheless, Falabellas are attractive and appealing, and are said to be intelligent, good-tempered and friendly horses when kept as pets. Their coat patterns vary, but the spotted Appaloosa-type coat pattern (see page 134) is increasingly sought-after.

Fell Pony

Height: **13-14 hh. (52-56 in.)**

Colors: **Black, brown bay, occasionally gray. Very few white markings.**

Use: **Saddle, harness**

Features: **Small head, broad across forehead and tapering down to muzzle; large open nostrils; luxurious mane and tail, left to grow long; powerful drive in hind legs because of strength and flexibility of hocks; feet are open at heels, with hard, blue horn and heels are feathered.**

Smaller and lighter than its close relation the Dales pony, the Fell pony comes from the northwestern edges of the Pennines, the rough moorlands of Westmorland and Cumberland. Both the Fell and the Dales ponies are descended from the same black Friesian stock brought to Britain by the Romans over 2,000 years ago, and used as auxiliary cavalry. Each breed, however, would develop slightly differently according to their habitat and to the work to which they were put.

The greatest influence on the Fell pony was of the swift-footed Galloway, the mount of the border raiders who harassed the Roman Legions, and later, that of the Scottish drovers. Although extinct since the 19th century, the Galloway, which was bred between Nithsdale and the Mull of Galloway, has left its mark in British ponies. It was strong, hardy, and very fast under saddle and harness, and could well have provided some of the 'running horse' stock that would become the basis for the eastern sires in the 17th and 18th century from which would spring the Thoroughbred (see page 122).

At first, however, the Fell pony (like the Dales) was a pack pony, carrying lead ore from the mines: the average load was 224 lb and the ponies travelled around 240 miles a week over some of the roughest land in Britain. But, because of its smaller size and better riding shoulders, the Fell pony was soon also used under saddle and harness, especially in local trotting races. In 1900 the Fell Pony Society was formed and the National Pony Society opened a section in its Stud Book: the strict rules and careful selection and line breeding of the strongest lines have ensured that very little 'foreign' blood has been introduced to the breed.

Consequently, the Fell is much sought-after in it own right for riding and driving, and, as a cross to produce horses of great competition potential.

Galiceno Pony

Height: **12–14 hh. (48-56 in.)**

Colors: **All solid colours**

Use: **Saddle, harness, ranch work,**

Features: **Almost pure white tail on palomino colored horses; Dun-colored horses have black mane, tail and dorsal list and sometimes zebra bars on lower limbs. Smooth gait; swift, running walk.**

The Galiceno pony from Mexico derives its name from the Spanish province of Galicia where it was first developed. Galicia is a region famed for its smooth-gaited horses which are distinguished by a very swift running walk. Its ancestors were the Portuguese Garrano (Minho) and Spanish Sorraia, probably brought to America by the Spanish from the island of Hispaniola (Haiti) in the 16th century. Both the Sorraia and Garrano stem from primitive stock such as the Tarpan, which contributed directly to the evolution of the Spanish horse.

Although referred to as a pony, and standing up to 14 hh, in its proportions and character, the Galiceno is really a small horse. Lightly built, the Galiceno has a fine head, large, well spaced eyes, upright shoulders, and a short back. Tough, intelligent, agile, and versatile, the Galiceno spread out of Mexico into the U.S.A. in the 1950s and since 1958, has been recognized as a breed. An attractive riding horse, with its characteristic, smooth gait of a fast running walk, the Galiceno is still widely used in Mexico in harness for farm work. Its hard feet and sound constitution are well adapted to working on hard, sun-baked soil.

Haflinger Pony

The Haflinger is a sturdy mountain breed that originated in the mountainous region of the Austrian Tyrol and which takes its name from the village of Hafling in the Etschlander Mountains where this pony was extensively bred. State studs were also established later at Piber and Ossiach, but today the principal Haflinger stud is at Jenesien where all stallions are owned by the Austrian state and all colt foals are subjected to rigorous inspection before being selected as potential future stallions.

The careful control of the breed and its mountain environment ensures a fixed type of pony, with an unmistakable – and very attractive – appearance: Haflingers are always chestnut or palomino with a beautiful flaxen mane and tail. They are powerfully built, being exceptionally muscular and strong in the loins, and the back. This combination of beauty and strength has led the ponies to be described as 'princes in front, peasants behind'! The Haflinger is sometimes known as the 'Edelweiss pony' as all Haflinger-bred ponies carry the brand mark of Austria's national flower with the letter H in the center.

The Haflingers breeding can be traced back to cold-blooded, now extinct Alpine

Height: up to 13.3 hh (53 in.)

Colors: Palomino, or chestnut with flaxen mane and tail

Use: Saddle, draught work, harness

Features: Characteristic color with flaxen mane and tail; Edelweiss brand on Halfing bred ponies; exceptionally free action with long striding walk.

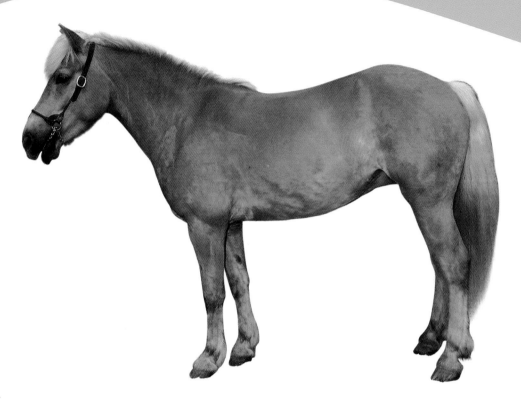

heavy horses and related pony breeds on one side, and to Arab (see page 113) origins on the other. Although a cold-blood itself, the modern pure-bred Haflinger can trace back to the Arab stallion El Bedavi XXII. This combination has produced a sure-footed, placid and hardworking pony that is ideal for draft, harness and riding work in rugged terrain. In Austria, young Haflingers are raised on the Alpine pastures – a practice known as 'Alpung' – where the thin but clean air helps to develop their strong lungs and hearts. They are not usually worked until they reach about four years old, but they have been known to work happily until they are 40, a testament to their strong constitutions.

The Italian 'version' of the Haflinger – and which also shares ancestry with El Bedawi XXII – is the Avelignese, bred in the Italian Alps and in the Apennine Mountains. Although the Avelignese is often bigger (around 14.2 hh/57 in.) and occasionally has white facial markings, in other respects the two breeds are almost identical in appearance.

Highland Pony

The largest and strongest of Britain's native ponies, the Highland is native to the north of Scotland and the Western Islands, although the ponies found on the mainland were larger and heavier than those found on the islands. This difference disappeared in the 19th century when Clydesdales (see page 99) were introduced to the islands to produce ponies that were strong enough for forestry work. (See also the Eriskay Pony, page 62).

Height: up to 14.2 hh. (57 in.)

Colors: Variety: duns in gray, yellow, gold, cream and fox; grays, browns, blacks, sometimes bays, sometimes 'bloodstone' (chestnuts with silver manes and tails); piebald also permitted

Use: Saddle, harness, pack

Features: Most have dorsal eel stripe; some have zebra markings on legs. Tails and manes are fine and silky touch. Feather ends in prominent tuft at fetlock.

The origins of the Highland pony appear to be prehistoric: after the Ice Age, ponies living in the far north of Scotland were derived from Pony Type 2 which resembled the Asiatic Wild Horse (see page 12), and possible crosses with Pony Type 1, which was similar to the Exmoor Pony (see page 109). Throughout its history however, there have been many outside influences on this original native stock to produce the modern Highland pony. In the Bronze Age, horses were imported from Scandinavia and later from Iceland, but the most significant contributions came in later, in the 16th–18th centuries. Around 1515, Louis XII of France gave King James V of Scotland a gift of horses – which included

the ancestors of the Percheron (see page 103). In the late 17th and early 18th centuries, the Clan Chief of Clanranald improved the ponies on Uist by importing Spanish horses. In 1870 century, a Norfolk Roadster type Hackney was brought to the Isles and had a particular influence on the ponies on the Isle of Arran. The MacNeils on the island of Barra introduced Arab blood to their stock, while John Munro-Mackenzie on the island of Mull used the Arab Syrian to develop the famous Calgary strain of ponies on the island.

Today, the Highland pony is an 'all-purpose' horse: free from hereditary diseases, it is long-lived and thrives on rough pasture, requiring little extra feed. Infinitely sure-footed, they are equally capable of crossing mountain passes and cross boggy land, while the placid nature of the Highland makes it ideal for use under saddle and in harness. Their incredible strength and stamina has also led them to be used as 'war horses' (they featured in the Jacobite Rebellions of the 18th century and in the Boer war in South Africa in the 19th century), for trekking and as pack horses. It is not unusual for a Highland pony to carry 252 lb – about the average weight of a deer carcass.

Icelandic Horse

Although the Icelandic horse stands no more than 13–13.2 hh, it is never referred to as a pony by the Icelanders. This is one of the toughest of the pony breeds: despite its small size it can easily carry a grown man at speed over great distances and over some of the roughest landscape in the world.

The horse was introduced into Iceland from Scandinavia, notably from Norway around AD 860, brought to the island by the two Norse chieftains Ingolfur and Leifur. These settlers and their horses were soon followed by others from the Norse colonies in the Western Isles of Scotland, Ireland and the Isle of Man. Interbreeding of this early stock gave rise to the Icelandic horse which for 1,000 years has received no outside blood. In AD 930, following a disastrous attempt to introduce eastern blood, the Althing (the world's oldest parliament) banned the import of horses into Iceland.

Even from this early date, selective breeding was being practised, using stallion fights as the basis for that selection. There were four types of Icelandic horse:

Height: **12–13 hh (48-52 in.)**
Colors: All, but primarily gray or dun
Use: Riding and harness work
Features: Heavy head; short, stocky body; deep girth; short back; very strong limbs with short cannons and strong hocks; peculiarly wedge shaped, sloping quarters but which are very strong and muscular; mane and tail are full; feathering on heels.

pack horses and draft horses; riding horses, and horses bred for meat. A more modern selective breeding began in 1879 in Skagafjordur, northern Iceland, which was based largely on the quality of the five gaits that are unique to the Icelandic horse. From this two distinct types emerged: the heavier chestnut color with the near white mane and tail, but breeding programs are based principally on the five gaits.

The five gaits are the *fetgangur* (walk) which is mostly used by pack animals; the *brokk* (trot), used when crossing rough country; the *stökk* (fast gallop), and the two very ancient gaits, the *skeið* (pace), a smooth, lateral gait, and the *tölt* (rack), a four-beat running walk used for crossing broken ground. In pacing races the Icelandic horse changes to the *skeið* after a 55 yd *stökk*.

pony used for draft and pack work, and the lighter type for riding. Both were used extensively in Iceland until the 1920s when they were the only forms of transport available. Because cattle cannot be wintered out in Iceland, horses are still bred for meat. Around half of Iceland's horses live out all year round in a semi-wild state with only the occasional supplement of herring to provide extra valuable nutrition.

There are no fewer than 15 basic color types and combinations of Icelandic horse – including palomino, skewbald and piebald – and some studs concentrate on breeding a preferred coat color. The Kirkjuber Stud produces the distinctive

New Forest Pony

This British breed, found in the New Forest in Hampshire, has one of the most varied genetic backgrounds — largely because of the accessible nature of their habitat. We know from the Forest Law of 1016 proclaimed by King Canute at Winchester that there were ponies in the forest, decades before the Norman kings exerted their powers over it.

Anyone travelling west through the south of England would pass through the New Forest, giving ample opportunity for the native ponies to cross with domestic stock.

After the Norman Conquest, King William Rufus (1087–1100) made the New Forest a royal hunting ground, preserving the deer and enforcing the Rights of Common Pasture for those people living within the forest. These 'Commoners' had — and continue to have — the right to run their ponies in the forest: today there are around 3,000 ponies running in the forest.

In the 13th century, in the first attempts to upgrade the breed, Welsh mares were turned out in the forest. While there may have been ongoing selective breeding by the

Height: **12.2–14 hh (49-56 in.)**
Colors: **All, except: piebald, skcwbald, and blue-eyed cream**
Use: **Saddle, harness**
Features: **Good, long sloping riding shoulders; long low action especially evident at the canter.**

Commoners in the following centuries, by the 19th century, the New Forest stock had degenerated so far that immediate action was required. Under the auspices of Lords Arthur Cecil and Lucas, Dartmoors, Exmoors, Highlands, Fells, Dales, Hackneys, Clydesdales, and Arabs were introduced in the New Forest. It was not until the end of World War II, however, that

there emerged five stallions that are recognized as the founding sires of the modern breed: Danny Denny, Goodenough, Brooming Slipon, Brookside David, and Knightwood Spitfire.

Some of the varied contributors to the modern breed can be detected in the New Forest pony: the heads are still rather horse-like, and there are often quite substantial variations in height : forest-bred ponies can be small, around 12–12.2 hh (48-49 in.) while stud-bred 'Foresters' can reach 14.2 hh (57 inches).

Nevertheless, the environment of the New Forest itself ensured that a pony of a distinctive 'type' was produced: water, marsh, and bog land are a feature of the New Forest moorland where the ponies live, and, while it provides a sufficient diet of coarse grasses, brambles, and gorse tips, food is never very plentiful. Consequently, theses conditions have contributed to the creation of a breed of strong-legged, sure-footed, and adaptable ponies with excellent riding shoulders and a distinctive, long, low action that is most evident at the canter.

Norwegian Fjord Pony

Height: **13–14.2 hh (52-57 in.)**
Colors: **Dun**
Use: **Saddle, harness, pack horse**
Features: **Distinctive upright, coarse mane with black hair at center and dorsal eel-stripe running from forelock to tip of tail; often zebra bar markings on the legs; tail is often silver, thick and full.**

Norway's dun colored Fjord pony bears a striking resemblance to the Asiatic Wild Horse (see page 12): it retains the uniform dun coat color, the dorsal eel-stripe running from forelock to the tip of the tail, and, it sometimes has zebra bar markings on its legs. In conformation the Fjord also retains its ancestor's short, compact form and overall strength and vigor. However, the modern Fjord does not have the convex profile seen in primitive stock.

The Fjord was the horse of the Vikings and accompanied them in their long boats to take part in raids: the first Norse raiders came from Hordaland, the chief habitat of the Fjord pony, and, consequently, its influence can be seen in Scotland's Highland pony (page 69) and in the ancient Icelandic horse.

The most notable feature of the Fjord is its coarse, erect mane – a characteristic of primitive equines. By ancient tradition, the mane is hogged (clipped) so that the black hairs at the center of the mane stand higher than the rest which are generally lighter, more silver in Color. The mane is cut in a crescent shape from poll to withers, giving the Fjord's neck a pronounced crest.

In Norway and beyond, it is highly regarded for its sure-footedness, stamina, and courage, and for its ability to work in hard terrain and in severe weather. It is used for plowing, as a pack pony, in harness, and under saddle.

Shetland Pony

Height: Traditionally, the Shetland is measured in inches, not hands: average is 38–40 inches

Colors: All colours: Black is foundation color, but brown, bay and gray as well as piebald and skewbald can be found

Use: Saddle, harness

Features: Very thick mane and tail to protect from weather; smooth coat in summer, wiry thick double coat growth in winter. Tough feet of hard, blue horn with pasterns that are sloped.

One of the world's most popular ponies and a favorite as a child's first mount, the Shetland pony has lived in the rugged and isolated Shetland and Orkney Islands situated 115 miles off the northeast coast of Scotland, for over 2,000 years. The smallest of Britain's native pony breeds, the Shetland lives on windswept islands with no trees, and where the soil is thin and acid, capable of supporting no more than rough grasses and heathers. These, along with mineral-rich seaweed found on the shoreline, form the staple diet of these small, but incredibly strong, ponies.

The most likely origins of the Shetland pony are in Scandinavia before the ice fields melted and left Britain isolated from continental Europe. The ponies left in the northernmost islands would have been tundra-type ponies: the Shetland, in fact, retains the extra large nasal cavities which allow for cold air to be warmed up sufficiently before it enters the lungs. Later, the Viking invaders brought their ponies and small, light-boned, active ponies can be seen in stone carvings dating from the 9th century on the islands of Burra and Bressay. These ponies, when compared to the human figures on the carvings, do not seem to have exceeded 40 inches in height.

Crofters on the islands have used the Shetland to work their land, and as a pack ponies, carrying seaweed and peat – the only source of fuel on islands with no wood available from trees – and as a means of transport. In 1847, an Act of Parliament

large populations, and each country operates its own stud books. In Argentina, the Shetland was the basis for the tiny Falabella (see page 63), while in North America, the Shetland has been crossed with the Hackney Pony to create the American Shetland, and, with the Appaloosa (see page 134) to produce the Pony of the Americas.

prohibited women and children working down coal mines: consequently, Shetland ponies were in great demand as pit ponies and a heavier, coarser pony was developed alongside the existing Shetland. Today, however, the breed is consistent in type: there has been a movement towards breeding 'miniature' Shetlands, which are even smaller than the general breed standard. With all such attempts at miniaturization there is the possibility that these Shetlands will loose their type.

The popularity of the Shetland has led to its export across the world: Canada, the United States, and Europe all have

Lundy Pony

Height: **Average 13.2 hh. (53 in.)**
Colors: **Cream, golden and dark dun, bright and dark bay, some black**
Use: **Saddle**
Features: **Symmetrical quarters; muscled yet elegant neck; neat head and alert expression.**

The granite stone Lundy Island is just 3½ miles long by ½ mile wide and is situated off the west coast of England where the Bristol Channel meets the Atlantic Ocean. The west side of the island is exposed to ferocious Atlantic gales, but the east side is more sheltered and supports a diverse range of flora and fauna, including the Lundy pony. The first ponies were brought to Lundy by the island's owner, Martin Coles Harman in 1928; these were New Forest ponies, which, after surviving the sea voyage, swam ashore to the island from the transport boat. A thoroughbred stallion was also part of the 'experiment' but he and his stock could not survive the rigors of the landscape and the harsh winters on the island. Subsequently, Welsh ponies (see page 85) and Connemara ponies (see page 54) were taken to the island. The Connemara cross proved to be the most successful and is responsible for the distinctive Lundy pony type although in the 1970s, New Forest stallions were once again used to 'experiment'.

Responsibility for the island herd – which now numbers around 20 ponies – is the Lundy Pony Preservation Society. The society is also responsible for the Lundy herd which is bred on mainland England where only Connemara stallions are used in the breeding program. On the island itself, the present Lundy stallion is the grandson of the Connemara stallion, Rosenharley Peadar.

The use of different stallions has resulted in a the mainland herd differing from the island herd in type and appearance: the island herd's colors are predominantly cream and golden dun, bright and dark bay, but the use of New Forest stallions led to the principal colors of dark dun and bay. The mainland herd retain the dark dun color as well as bright bay, but some black coats also appear. In both instances though, the compact body and strong loins, overall conformation and robust constitution have made for a pony ideal for riding and with show-jumping potential.

Polo Pony

Height: **15–15.3 hh (50-61 in.)**
Colors: **Any**
Use: **Sport**
Features: **Hard, strong feet; hard joints and strong back; fearless and quite aggressive; nimble, very fast and with great stamina.**

The Polo pony is not a breed in the strict sense of the word but more a fixed type that evolved with the game itself as it spread westwards into Europe from Asia. The game of polo originated in Persia about 2,500 years ago where it was known as *Chaugan*, which means 'mallet', but its present name is derived from the Tibetan word *pulu* meaning 'root', from which the polo ball was made. Moslem invaders from the northwest and Chinese from the northeast took the game to India where, in the mid-19th century, English tea planters in Assam discovered the game.

Silchar, the capital of the Cacher district became the birthplace of the modern polo game, and the oldest polo club (the Silchar Club, founded in 1859). Originally teams had nine riders, but then these were reduced to seven, and later to four as the ponies became bigger and faster.

The ponies on which the English originally played in India were from Manipur state, between Assam and Burma, and which stood no taller than 12.2 hh (49 in.). By the 1870s, though, the ponies were getting bigger and the height limit was set in 1876 at 13.2 hh (43 in.) in India and 14.2 hh (57 in.) in England. In 1916, the height ruling was abolished, largely due to pressure from American players (the game was introduced to the U.S.A. in 1878) and from then the height increased to the modern 15–15.3 hh (60-61 in.). The modern polo pony is therefore a small horse – although it is always called a pony.

The game is largely dominated by Argentinean ponies, which are the result of crosses between Thoroughbreds and the native Criollo (see page 148) and then putting the progeny back to Thoroughbred. The result is a lean, wiry pony with exceptionally strong limbs and very hard strong feet – necessary since the game is played at full gallop on very hard ground.

Pre-match preparations for the ponies are meticulous and designed to protect the ponies: they involve hogging the mane and plaiting the tail into a neat polo bang so that the stick does not get caught; fitting protective bandage 'boots' onto all four legs, and, extremely careful inspection of the saddlery so that accidents do not occur during play. A draw rein allows the rider to control the pony's head by 'drawing' it inwards while a gag bit raises the head: the degree to which the pony's head can be raised is governed by a martingale.

British Spotted Pony

Height: up to 14.2 hh (57 in.)

Colors: Leopard, blanket, snowflake, few spot

Use: Saddle

Features: All British Spotted ponies must display some of the following: white scherla round the eye; mottled skin; striped hooves. Action is low and straight from the shoulder, hocks well flexed with straight action coming well under the body though cob types may display more knee action.

The spotted coat patterns of horses and ponies developed as a form of protective camouflage and are likely to have emerged in prehistoric times. There is very early evidence of spotted horses in the beautiful cave paintings at Lascaux and Pech-Merle in France painted in around 18,000 BC. These are probably the distant relatives of today's spotted breeds. Most spotted breeds share the characteristic of the white sclera round the eyes – similar to that of humans – a mottled skin (particularly evident around the muzzle and genitalia), and distinctive striped feet.

Throughout the centuries, imports of foreign blood into Britain have played their part in shaping the character of native breeds: 2,000 years ago the Roman army brought with them many elegant spotted horses from Spain. Because of their unusual appearance, spotted ponies were highly prized: in a parchment from 1298 listing all the horses purchased for Edward I for use in his campaign at Falkirk, Scotland, a spotted Welsh Cob (see page 84) from Powys, Wales purchased from one Robin Fitzpayne, is the most expensive of all. Later, spotted ponies and horses came to Britain by way of 'diplomatic' gifts between monarchs, and even, in the 20th century, as circus performers.

There are numerous recognized coat patterns of British Spotted Pony,: 'leopard' is spots of any color on a white or light colored background; 'blanket' is an area of

white over the hips or hindquarters (with or without spots). The base can be any color and the blanket can extend over the entire back and shoulders. 'Snowflake' consists of white spots on a dark base coat: this color can appear to be almost roan, but in the British Spotted, there are often varnish marks to distinguish it from 'ordinary' roan. 'Few spot' is distinguished by groupings of dark hairs within an area – usually the nose, cheekbones, stifle, gaskin, and knee. In the British Spotted Pony breed standard, piebald and skewbald are not permitted, although solid colors are eligible for entry to a separate breed register so long as they

are of proven Spotted breeding and preferably, show some of the other characteristics of the breed mentioned above.

In 1947 the British Spotted Horse and Pony Society was formed to keep a register and to preserve the breed. In 1976, the society split: ponies under 14.2 hh were looked after by the British Spotted Pony Society, while larger ones were entered into the British Appaloosa Society registers. Over the years the British Spotted Pony has regrettably become a rare breed: only 800 or so ponies are currently registered in the society's stud books.

Welsh Cob

Height: No smaller than 14.2 hh (57 in.)
Colors: All solid colors
Use: Saddle, harness
Features: Short muscular legs; high knee action;
dished face with large eyes and wide, open
nostrils.

The Welsh Cob is the largest of the Welsh breeds and, uniquely for British ponies, has no upper height limit for showing purposes.

The heartland of the Welsh Cob is Cardiganshire where the breed derived from crosses of Welsh Mountain Ponies with Roman imports and Spanish and Barb-type horses introduced in the 11th and 12th centuries. These resulted in the famous Powys Cob – the mount of the English armies from the 12th century onwards – and the now extinct Welsh Cart Horse. In the 19th century, mixes of Powys Cob stock with Norfolk Roadsters and Yorkshire Coach Horses were also made, but in the end, the Welsh Cob remains essentially a larger version of the Welsh Mountain Pony.

The Welsh Cob is famed for its great powers of endurance, its trotting ability and its performance in harness. In the past it was in great demand as a gun horse and for mounted infantry. A naturally good jumper, the Welsh Cob also makes an excellent hunter, while a Thoroughbred cross – especially a second cross – produces excellent competition horses of size, ability, and speed. Before stallion licensing was introduced, breeding stock was selected in the traditional manner in Wales: on the basis of performance over a given distance.

Welsh Mountain Pony

Height: **12 hh (48 in.) max**
Colors: **All except piebald and skewbald**
Use: **Saddle**
Features: **Crested neck; tiny, pointed ears; tail high
set and carried high; short powerful loin and
compact body; exceptionally hard feet of
blue horn .**

The smallest of Welsh pure breeds, the Welsh Mountain Pony has roamed the mountains and moorlands of Wales for centuries, although over the years, out-crosses have been introduced. Julius Caesar formed an Imperial Roman stud at Bala in Merionethshire and introduced oriental blood to upgrade the stock. In the 19th century there were infusions of Arab blood and from the now extinct Norfolk Roadster (a predecessor of the Hackney, see page 167). The first recorded influence however came from the Thoroughbred Merlin, a direct descendent of the Darley Arabian, who was turned out onto the Ruabon Hills in Clywd in the 18th century: his influence was such that today, such ponies in Wales are still called 'merlins'.

The modern Welsh Mountain Pony, the base from which the Welsh Pony and Welsh Cobbs evolved, is very distinctive in its appearance and is noted for its uniquely powerful action, its intelligence and its hereditary hardiness. The legs are slender and elegant, with short cannons and flat, well formed joints and dense bones. The breed should also have what is called a 'bread basket': depth through the girth and a well-ribbed middle.

A superb riding pony and exceptional in harness as well, the Welsh Mountain Pony is one of the world's most popular ponies, and, as a foundation in breeding bigger ponies and horses, it passes on its invaluable strengths and qualities.

Heavy Horses

More than a century after the invention of the internal combustion engine and two centuries since steam was harnessed as a source of energy, we continue to measure the power of an engine against the horse. This is not surprising when we realize that until the end of the 18th century, the horse was really the only source of motive power available.

Undoubtedly, the first role of the horse was as a pack animal, used to carrying whatever man required to sustain his life.

Without such pack horses, local, national, and international trade would never have been possible as trading would have been largely confined to coastal regions where ships could safely dock. Pack horses provided the means by which raw materials and manufactured goods produced inland could reach these ships which could then take them across the world.

With the development of the yoke in the Bronze Age (around 5000 years BC in the Middle East and 2000 years BC in Europe),

A FINE NORIKER STALLION.

ONE OF THE MOST POPULAR HORSES – THE SHIRE.

a horse could effectively pull more weight than it could carry, and so began the long history of horse-drawn vehicles starting with the chariot and simple carts.

Heavy horses are the gentle giants of the equine world and can stand up to 18.2 hh. Immensely powerful and strong, they have deeper chests and shorter, thicker legs than warm bloods of the same height. Today's heavy horses are the descendants of the medieval knights' war horse or destrier. Although large and powerful, these ancient horses would still have been smaller than

today's breeds but were capable of carrying a fully armored knight weighing about 300 lb. Add on the weight of the saddle and the caparison, and the horse still had enough power to provide momentum for the knight's lance which was anything up to 15 ft long.

Since the Middle Ages the destriers' descendants have been bred for their power and size as draft horses. In one way or another, all horses 'work', but a distinction can be made between those horses which are employed for recreational purposes, and those horses which are employed directly in 'industry', in particular, in agriculture. Heavy horses powered the earliest 'mass transit' systems: first, pulling stage coaches up and down the country linking towns and cities together, then, pulling the canal barges, buses and trams. The first railway in Britain opened in 1803 between Croydon and Wandsworth in south London and used horse-drawn carriages; heavy horses continued to be used in railway shunting yards until 1967 when Europe's last shunting horse was retired in Newmarket, Cambridgeshire, England.

The heavy horses also still went to war until World War I but were used as draft horses rather than chargers. Heavy horses pulled the enormous guns into position, hauled supplies, and drew ambulances. While many heavy horses continue to work as draft horses, especially those employed by breweries to both pull their dray carts and to advertize their heritage, the military role today of heavy horses is thankfully confined to the purely ceremonial, as regimental drum horses.

The cold bloods, or heavy horses, were part of everyday life on farms and towns all over Europe until quite recently, and indeed, in some parts of northern and eastern Europe, these horses remain essential to effective farming.

THE HEAVY CLYDESDALE HORSE

The use of heavy horses in agriculture did not occur until the 18th century: only then did the heavy horse supplant teams of oxen in much of the world, and today these continue to provide the main sources of power in Asia and the Far East. But it was the availability of heavy horses that allowed for the development of the sophisticated horse-drawn machinery that encouraged the 'industrialization' of agriculture from the 18th century onwards until motorization took over. In the prairies of the United States, the use of horses meant that millions of acres of land could be put to the plow: huge combine harvesters drawn by 40-horse teams controlled by six men were common, while the methods of harnessing were such that one man alone could drive a team of 36 horses to a set of harrows or drills.

A LOVELY CHESTNUT SUFFOLK PUNCH.

89

Shire

Height: 16–18 hh (64–72 in.)

Colors: Black, bay, brown, gray with white markings

Use: Heavy draft, showing

Features: Average girth of a Shire stallion is 6–8 ft ; short back; powerful loins; legs are clean and muscular with flat bone of 11–12 in; feet are open and big round the top of coronet; heavy feathers but always straight and silky.

Considered by many as the supreme heavy horse, the Shire takes its name from its traditional breeding ground in the English shire counties of Lincoln, Leicester, Stafford, and Derby. The Shire descends from the great medieval war horse, or destrier, (from the Latin word *dextrarius*, meaning 'right sided' because the knight only mounted his horse just before battle was joined, otherwise it was led from the right, by his squire). This was sometimes called the 'Great Horse', but later became known as the 'English Black Horse' when Oliver Cromwell, Lord Protector of England during the brief period in the 17th century when England was a commonwealth, bestowed the name. Black continues to be the most popular color of the Shire, but brown, bay, and gray, with silky, straight, and abundant white feathers, are also to be found.

The main influence on the evolution of the massive Shire — which can weigh between 20 and 22 cwt (2,2240–2,688 lb) — was the Flemish, or Flanders Horse. During the 16th and 17th centuries, large numbers of these were brought to England with Dutch contractors employed to drain the Fenlands in the eastern counties of England in order to increase the amount of available agricultural land, and these Flanders Horses were crossed with native stock. The enormous power of these horses can be seen in the weight-pulling records: in 1924 at the Wembley Exhibition, a pair of Shires pulling against a dynamometer (a device for measuring mechanical power) exceeded the maximum reading and were

estimated at pulling equal to a starting load of 50 tonnes. The same pair, driven in tandem on wet granite sets, shifted 18.5 tonnes – with the shaft horse starting the pull before the leader had even got into his collar!

The foundation stallion of the Shire breed is recognized as the Packington Blind Horse, who stood at Ashby-de-la-Zouch, Leicestershire, between 1755 and 1770. He was black and his name appears first in the stud book in 1878 published by the English Cart Horse Society. The name Shire was not used until 1884, however, when the society changed its name to the Shire Horse Society. An indication of their widespread use is born out by the fact that between 1901 and 1914, some 5,000 Shires were registered each year and the breed enjoyed a thriving export market, particularly to the U.S.A. After World War II,

there was little need for Shires in either industry or agriculture and their numbers dropped significantly.

Shires were, however, still in employed by many breweries, and their continued existence is largely due to the loyal support of this industry. The Shires can be seen today pulling the brewery drays in many cities and towns where they always turn heads and are real 'traffic stoppers' in their majesty. At the annual Horse of the Year Show in England, the spectacular Drive of the Heavy Horses is one of the most popular events, while the annual Shire Horse Show at Peterborough, Cambridgeshire, attracts an average of 300 entries and over 15,000 spectators. In an age of technology and urban living, hundreds still turn out regularly to country shows to watch and cheer Shires and their handlers in plowing competitions.

Ardennais

Height: 15.3 hh (61.2 in.) and above

Colors: Roan is preferred, accompanied by pale, blonde mane, but also red-roan, gray, dark chestnut, and brown. Light chestnuts and palominos are permitted but black is not.

Use: Heavy draft, also bred for meat

Features: Massive, straight profile head; squared-off muzzle; prominent eye sockets; small, pricked ears; broad and unusually short back; unusually for heavy breeds, the withers in line with, or even lower than, the croup; short, very strong legs.

The ancient Ardennes breed of heavy horse belongs to both France and Belgium, and it is almost certain that it is a direct descendant of the prehistoric horses whose remains were found at Solutre: the modern Ardennais still has the same primitive skeletal formation of the head and the distinctive, squared-off nose. The breed was know to the ancient Greek historian Herodotus (c.484-425 BC) who praised them for their hardiness and stamina, and to Julius Caesar. Stocky and compact, with very large bones, the Ardennais was well suited to the Ardennes region, where the severe climate continues to produce excellent horses of medium height ideally suited to farm work.

Before the 19th century, the Ardennais was a less massive horse that was both ridden and used for light draft work. During the French Revolution (1789) and in the Empire years following, they were regarded as the finest artillery horses in Europe. In 1812, during Napoleon's disastrous assault on Moscow, they were the only horses tough enough to withstand the severe Russian winter during the retreat, and were responsible for bringing home the greater part of the Emperor's wagon train. Descendants of these lighter Ardennes 'Postier' or 'post horses' could still be found around Bassigny, in northeast France, until as recently as the 1970s.

The modern Ardennes is the result of 19th century breeding: to increase its speed and stamina, crosses were made with Arab (see page 113) blood. Later, crosses were made with Percheron (see page 103), Boulonnais, and Thoroughbred (see page 122). Three types of Ardennes horse emerged: a small, older-type Ardennais of around 15–16 hh (60-64 in.); the bigger and more massive Ardennais du Nord, also known as the Trait du Nord, which resulted from out-crosses with the Brabant or Belgian Heavy Draft Horse (and which can also be found in Belgian as the Belgian Ardennes Horse); and, the Auxois, the larger and most powerful version of the original Ardennais, found mostly in the Burgundy region in northeastern France.

The Ardennais today is stocky and thick set — more so than any other heavy horse — and has an unusually short back. It has been described as being 'built like a tractor' and as having legs 'like small oak trees'. The feet are surprisingly small, are lightly feathered, and not as thick as many other breeds. The ears are also small and pricked, which is also unusual in a heavy breed. The neck is immensely strong and heavy. Extraordinarily hardy, the Ardennais is also very docile and gentle, to the extent that they can be handled by children. As well as being used for heavy draft work, the Ardennais is also bred for its meat.

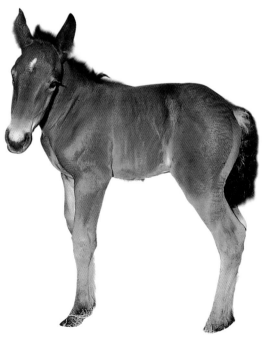

Boulonnais

Height: 16-16.3 hh (64-65 in.)
Colors: Usually gray, but bay and chestnuts are also to be found
Use: Draft work
Features: Fine head on short, thick but gracefully arched neck; muscular shoulders and powerful chest; broad, straight back; strong legs; large, solid joints; bushy mane and tail.

A native of northwest France, the Boulonnais, widely held by many to be the 'noblest' of all the draft breeds, is a descendant of the ancient north European heavy horse. These were crossed in the first century BC with horses of eastern origin said to have been from Julius Caesar's Numidian cavalry that invaded Britain in 55-54 BC. Later in the Middle Ages further oriental blood was introduced to the breed during the Crusades.

Crosses with German heavy horses in the 14th century gave greater weight and size to the breed. When the Spanish occupied the Low Countries in the 16th century, Spanish blood was introduced which improved the constitution and action of the horses, and by the 17th century, the breed was established and called the Boulonnais. Two distinct types emerged: the smaller Boulonnais stood between 15.1 and 15.3

hh (61-62 in.) and was known as the mareeur or mareyeur (the 'horse of the tide'). It had an energetic trotting pace which made it ideally suited for the speedy carriage of fish from Boulogne to Paris.

While the smaller 'horse of the tide' no longer exists, the second, heavier type of Boulonnais used for draft work, continues to thrive. The action of the Boulonnais is exceptional in a draft horse: straight, long, and swift. The influence of its eastern ancestors is clearly visible in the straight profile of the head, the arched neck, the well-proportioned physique, and the peculiarly bushy tail which is set high in the quarters.

Breton

Height: Draft Breton: 16 hh (64 in.),
Breton Postier: 15 hh (60 in.)
Colors: Blue and red roan, chestnut, bay, gray,
Use: Draft work
Features: Square head with straight profile; short,
thick arched neck running into short shoulders;
broad, strong body; strong quarters; short, very
strong and muscular limbs.

Since the Middle Ages, Brittany has been famed for its distinctive types of horse which were derived from a 'hairy' little horse from the Black Mountains in the west of Brittany, possibly a descendant of the Steppe Horse. At one time there were four distinct types, but today, two types of Breton are recognized. The first is the heavy draft horse which is the result of crosses with Boulonnais, Percheron (see page 103), and in the mountain areas, with the massive Ardennes, which produced a stronger and heavier animal. In the mid-19th century, Norfolk Roadster blood was introduced and the result was the second Breton type, the Postier, which was the ideal horse for light draft work. The Postier is a more compact, almost clean legged and lighter version of the Suffolk Punch (see page 104) and its action and constitution are very energetic and extremely sound. In common with the customs of other French draft breeds, the Breton's tail is docked which prevents the reins from becoming caught up under the tail.

Still an immensely popular horse in France, the Breton is exported worldwide both as a working animal and for breeding.

Gypsy Vanner

Height: 14–15.2 hh (56-61 in.)
Colors: Piebald, skewbald, other colors accepted
Use: Draft work, traditionally, hauling gypsy caravans
Features: Long, flowing manes, tails and feathers make horses look as if they are 'flying' when they run.

The relationship between gypsies and their horses is legendary, but the Gypsy Vanner Horse is a 'modern' breed: the registry was created only in 1996 in the United States where Dennis and Cindy Thompson imported the first specimens – two fillies called Bat and Dolly. Gypsy Vanner horses are colorful, compact horses with magnificent flowing manes, tails, and feathers. When they run, their hair streams out and it appears as though the horses are flying! On average the horses are between 14 and 15.2 hh and the short neck and back give the horse its power to pull the gypsy caravans.

Developed in eastern Europe over the centuries, the Gypsy Vanner is the result of Friesian (see page 160), Shire (see page 90), Clydesdale (see page 99), and Dales Pony (see page 56) crosses to produce a horse that had plenty of stamina, a calm temperament, and since it was sound and easy to maintain, one that was ideally suited to a travelling lifestyle. Heavy-boned, with flat knees and ample hooves, most Gypsy Vanner Horses are piebald (black and white) or skewbald (brown and white), although the breed society recognizes all colors. The mission of the Gypsy Vanner Horse Society is to honor and respect the standards established in the oral tradition of the Gypsy communities in the pursuit of the perfect caravan horse.

Comtois

Height: **14.3-15.3 hh (48-62 in.)**
Colors: **Usually bay or chestnut with a flaxen mane**
Use: **Light draft work**
Features: **Square head with a straight profile; small, mobile ears; short muscular neck; moderately well defined withers; straight back; wide, sloping croup; low set tail; deep, wide chest; long, sloping shoulders; slender but strong legs, with a tendency to sickle hocks; ample feathering; solid feet.**

The Comtois is an ancient breed of heavy horse form the Franche-Comté region. A medieval war horse, it became renowned as a cavalry and artillery horse, employed by both Louis XIV and Napoleon.

In the 19th century, the Comtois was bred with other draft breeds and since 1905, a much stronger horse with improved legs has been produced using small Ardennais sires. This later influence can also be observed in the free action of the Comtois. Today, the Comtois is bred in the Massif Central, the Pyrenees, and the Alps. Sure-footed, active and very hardy horses, Comtois are still employed for hauling wood or pulling sleighs at ski resorts. The Comtois is also exported to North Africa for agricultural use, and is used for meat production.

A lightly built draft horse, the Comtois can be found in shades of chestnut with a contrasting, light flaxen mane and tail.

Norman Cob

Height: 15.3 -16.2 hh
(61-65 in.)
Colors: Chestnut, bay
Use: Light draft
Features: Powerful and stocky frame without the
massiveness of the true heavy breeds. Crested
neck; compact body; powerful quarters with tail
set high; short legs; medium sized feet.

The Norman Cob is descended from the ancient small Norman and Breton horses known as *bidets*. The Romans crossed them with their heavy pack mares to produce a strong utility horse, and by the Middle Ages, Norman breeders were famed for their war horses which were ideal as light draft horses. In the 16th and 17th century however, the breed became lighter as a result of out-crosses to Arab and Barb horses. In the 19th century, further crosses with Thoroughbreds, Norfolk Roadsters, and 'half-bred' English 'hunter' stallions led to the development of the Anglo-Norman, which developed into the Selle Français.

At the beginning of the 20th century, a distinction was made between the lighter Norman horses of riding or cavalry type, and the sturdier, heavier horses that could be used as light draft horses. These draft horses retained the energetic paces of their ancestors, in spite of becoming heavier over the years. With docked tails, they were called 'cobs', and were recognized as a breed in their own right.

Clydesdale

The Clydesdale is Scotland's only extant heavy horse. It originated in the Clyde Valley in Lanarkshire as a result of crossing local mares with heavier Flemish stallions which were imported at the beginning of the 18th century. The breed was essentially founded between 1715-1720 by the 6th Duke of Hamilton and the breeder John Paterson of Lochlyloch whose interest was in producing strong draft horses suitable for agricultural work and for hauling coal from the newly opened mines in Lanarkshire. Consequently, great emphasis has always been given to breeding individuals with very sound legs and good feet. The feet are large, rather flat, but very open with well formed frogs, and are ideally suited to work on very hard surfaces like city streets. However they are less well suited to plowing as they can be too large to fit neatly into the furrow! Nevertheless, the Clydesdales worked the prairies of Canada and America and can claim to be the 'breed that built Australia'.

In the 19th century, Shires (see page 90) were also extensively crossed-in by notable breeders such as Lawrence Drew, steward to the 11th Duke of Hamilton at Merryton, and David Riddell, who also set up the

Height: 16.2–18 hh (65-72 in.)
Colors: Usually bay or brown, but black, gray and roan also appear. Heavy white markings on face and legs, and on underside of body are general.
Use: Heavy draft work, ceremonial
Features: 'Cow hocks' (the hind legs placed close together) are a breed characteristic and hind legs are longer than in many other heavy breeds; straight profile to head; shoulders more sloped and neck proportionately longer than a Shire's.

Select Clydesdale Horse Society in 1883 (in direct opposition to the official Clydesdale Horse Society Stud Book which had been published in 1878). In spite of Shire influence, the Clydesdale has retained its lighter build.

The Clydesdale is now distinctive in both type and appearance: the legs often appear to be long and carry an abundance of silky feather; the joints are big and the hocks broad, with cow hocks viewed not as a fault but as a characteristic of the breed. The Clydesdale is also famed for its action, described by the Clydesdale Horse Society as 'a flamboyant style, a flashy spirited bearing and a high stepping action that makes him a singularly elegant animal among draft horses'. Such a delight to watch, it has been said that the Clydesdale 'turns an ordinary beer delivery into a public event' and no mounted military parade in Britain would be complete without a Clydesdale drum horse. The Clydesdale is a also one of the most popular heavy horses across the world and can be found in continental Europe, Russia, South Africa, Japan, Australia, and New Zealand, as well in the U.S.A. and Canada.

Noriker

The Noriker takes its name from the ancient kingdom of Noricum which was a vassal state of the Roman Empire. Its borders were about the same as those of modern day Austria, the home of the Noriker. Across the southern borders were the Venetii, who had been established there since 900 BC and were famed for their horse breeding: this would become the native land of the Haflinger (see page 67) and it seems likely that the Noriker owes something to these mountain ponies.

In the mountainous landscape of Austria, the Romans required war horses that could also be used as pack and draft animals.

Height: **15–17hh (60-68 in.)**
Colors: **Distinct color lines recognized include: dapple and brindle coat patterns; black-headed dapple gray; brown; shades of chestnut; Marbach horses have liver-chestnut color with flaxen mane and tail**
Use: **Harness, saddle**
Features: **Hind legs marked by strong second gaskins; great depth at the girth – often exceeds measurement from elbow to ground; heavy squared head tapering to muzzle.**

The Norikers were first bred by the Romans at Juvavum, near Salzburg, but from the Middle Ages onward, it was the monasteries that were to be the most significant contributors to the formation of the breed, and the finest specimens were to be found in the Gross Glockner area. In 1565 under monastic control, the breed characteristics were regularized and improved and under the Prince-Archbishop of Salzburg, the Salzburg Stud Book was established, new stud farms developed and standards laid down. Later, Spanish, Neapolitan and Burgundian stallions were introduced to improve the breed. This introduction of new blood not only increased the size of the Noriker, but by the 18th century, resulted in the spotted coat pattern that is particularly evident in

the horses from the Pinzgau district, called Pinzgauer-Norikers.

In addition to the Pinzgauer, the Salzburg Stud Book recognizes four other principal Noriker strains: Kartner (Corinthian), Tiroler (Tyrolean), Steier, and Bavarian – also called the South German Coldblood. At Marbach in Württemberg, is Germany's oldest state-owned stud where the typical strain of Noriker in the traditional liver-chestnut coat color with flaxen mane and tail is bred. Because of its role in forestry work locally, this Noriker is known as the Black Forest Horse.

All Norikers must meet the strict conformational breed standards and furthermore, are performance tested: stallions are tested before being used at stud, and have to undergo the normal test to prove willingness in harness – the ability to pull a heavy load, to walk 500 yards and to trot 1,000 yards in a given time. Mares, are also subject to testing when they carry their first foals. The resulting breed is a compact, strong, versatile heavy horse suited to working in mountains that is also noted for its gentle and willing temperament.

Percheron

Height: 16–17 hh (64-68 in.)
Colors: Gray, black
Use: Draft
Features: Feet of hard blue horn, no feathers at heels; straight profile to head with long ears, prominent eyes, and, flat nose with very wide, open nostrils; neck is long and arched.

Owing much to its oriental blood, the elegant Percheron hails from the Le Perche region in Normandy. Only those horses bred in the French Departments of Le Perche (Sarth, Eur et Loire, Loir et Cher, and Orne) are admitted into the Percheron Stud Book, while those bred in other regions have their own stud books.

Percheron ancestors apparently carried the Frankish knights of Charles Martel at the Battle of Poitiers in 732 AD when they defeated the invading Moors. Consequently, the Arab or Barb horses of the enemy influenced the breed, and oriental blood was also imported following the First Crusade.

The Percheron has served as a war horse, as a stage coach horse, and as a farm horse; it pulled heavy artillery during World War I, and was also an immensely popular breed overseas. In the 1880s some 5,00 stallions and 2,500 mares were exported to the United States alone, with significant numbers also sent to South Africa and Australia. The percheron has the advantage over many other breeds in that it adapts easily to different climatic conditions, and, it is an excellent base stock for crossing. It is a hardy, even-tempered, powerful, and versatile horse.

Suffolk Punch

Height: **16-16.3 hh (64-65 in.)**
Colors: **Chestnut**
Use: **Heavy draft, showing**
Features: **Longevity; short powerful legs with little feathering; huge, rounded quarters; girth can measure up to 6 ft 8 in.; strongly crested neck; broad forehead; ears are relatively small for a heavy horse.**

As their name implies, the Suffolk Punch originated in the county of that name, but, for generations they have been regarded as natives of the entire East Anglian region. The Suffolk Punch can be traced back to the 16th century: William Camden in his *Britannia* (published in 1586) refers to the breed as having been in existence since 1505, and, no doubt the trotting Norfolk Roadsters and the heavier Flanders mares imported in the

16th century played a part in their development. Both possessed the same coloring now regarded as characteristic of the Suffolk, and the Flanders Horses were also competent trotters.

The Suffolk Punch is one of the purest of the British heavy breeds: every individual today can trace its descent from one stallion, Thomas Crisp's Horse of Ufford (Orford), stud book number 404, which was foaled in 1768. This stallion was used in the area around Woodbridge, Saxmundham, and Framlingham, where Suffolk Punch breeding is still centered. Crisp's horse was described as large-bodied, short-legged, bright 'chestnut' – spelled then without the 't' – and standing 15.2 hh. All Suffolks today are chestnut, but seven shades are recognized by the Suffolk Horse Society, formed in 1877 by Herman Biddell: these range from a pale, almost mealy color, to a dark, almost brown shade, but the most usual shade is the bright reddish chestnut color.

The Suffolk Punch was developed as a farm horse and is well suited to working the heavy soils of East Anglia, for it is both clean-legged and possesses great pulling power and stamina. The quarters are of great strength, but the hind legs are placed close together to allow the horse to walk a 9-inch furrow. The Suffolk also notably thrives on less feed than other heavy horses: typically in East Anglia the horses were fed only once, at 4.30 am and then went to the fields at 6.30 am, where they worked with short rests until 2.30 pm. Other heavy breeds required a mid-morning break and second feed followed by a digestion period.

The success of the Suffolk Punch owes much to careful selective breeding by East Anglian farmers and to Biddell's strict rules adopted by the Breed Society for registration and sales: no animal could be shown at any of the leading agricultural shows or sold at the Society's sales without a vet's certification of soundness. At fairs where Punches were offered for sale, they were tested by being hitched to a heavy, fallen tree: the horse did not need to move the tree, but was required to get right down on his knees in the typical Suffolk drawing attitude in order to pass the test.

American Cream Draft

Height: 15-16.3 hh (60-65 in.)
Colors: Cream
Use: Draft
Features: Amber eyes, white mane and tail, pink skin

The American Cream Draft horse is the only breed of draft horse to originate in the United States of America. Strictly of draft breeding the American Cream is not to be confused with the American Crème (which is a color type), Palominos, or other 'light' breeds.

Sometime around the beginning of the 20th century, Harry 'Hat' Lakin, from Ellsworth, Hamilton County, Iowa, purchased a cream-colored mare from a farm sale in nearby Story County, Iowa.

This little mare was called 'Old Granny' and she was to become the foundation dam of 98% of all the horses now registered with the American Cream Draft Association. Old Granny's description was also to become the standard by which breeders worked to maintain the breed: a rich, cream color; white mane and tail, pink skin, and amber-colored eyes.

Old Granny raised several cream colts on the Lakin farm before being sold to neighbors, the Nelson Brothers. It was Eric Christian, a vet from Jewell who, having noticed one of Old Granny's stallion colts, persuaded the Nelsons to keep him. This stallion was to be called Nelson's Buck No. 2 and is now regarded as the progenitor of the breed: he sired one cream stallion, Yancy No. 3 in 1923, out of a big Percheron (see page 103) mare also owned by the Nelsons.

By 1935, interest in the American Cream Draft was growing and it was due to C.T Rierson, the owner of Ardmore Stock Farm, near Radcliffe, Hardin, Iowa, who had Percherons and Aberdeen Angus cattle, that first thoughts were given to developing this new breed and from then on, accurate records of breeding and subsequent

offspring were recorded. Soon other interested breeders were involved: H.L. Bavender and E.E. Reece of New Providence, Iowa; Verner Stromer of Klemme, Iowa; Ray Veldhouse and Gaylord Engle were the founding breeders who set the scene and encouraged new breeders to concentrate their efforts on improving and perfecting the breed they established. In the spring of 1944, at Iowa Falls, Iowa, a group of interested breeders met and formed the American Cream Draft Horse Association; in 1950, the breed was recognized by the Iowa Department of Agriculture.

By carefully selecting and mating the best individuals by line breeding and with the best bloodlines of other draft breeds, the size and quality of these magnificent horses has been improved without loss of their type and characteristics. The ideal American Cream Draft is a rich, medium cream color, with a white mane and tail and pink skin – which is essential for the cream coat. Some white markings are also highly desirable in the breed, and the beautiful, amber-colored eyes are also an unusual and distinguishing feature of the breed. Foal are born with nearly white eyes, but they darken soon afterwards. A medium heavy draft horse, the ideal mature size and weight is 15–16 hh and 1,600 lb (for females), and, 16–16.3 hh and 1,800–2,000 lb for stallions.

Light Horses

The world's light horses are founded on breeds that are largely 'eastern' in origin: the Arab, the Barb (of North Africa), the Thoroughbred (an Arab derivative), and the Spanish Horse (itself influenced greatly by the Barb). Arabs, Barbs, and Thoroughbreds are known as 'hot bloods', a name which reflects the intense 'purity' of their breeding, while other light horses are known as 'warmbloods' and these stand between 15 and 17.2 hh (60-69 inches). Their conformation – a narrow frame, long legs, and sloping shoulders – makes them suitable for

A POLICE HORSE.

riding. Most light horses are fast and agile and many are prized for their qualities of endurance: the so-called 'desert horses' such as the Akhal-Teke (see page 124) are famous for their stamina.

Horse breeds and types originally developed very gradually over time by adapting to both their natural environments and through interrelations with groups of horses sharing the same regional homelands. But when the horse became domesticated, human intervention meant that there was a rapid increase in 'deliberate' breeding to produce specific types and breeds of horses. The practice of gelding male horses meant that breeding could only be carried on from the best stock and this in turn increased the quality and accentuated the characteristics that were most suited to the type of activity in which the horses were engaged. With developments in agricultural techniques and productivity, more nutritious foodstuffs meant that horses became faster, bigger, and/or stronger as breeders required.

From the earliest days of domestication it is likely that horses were used in sport: horse racing, either in harness or under saddle, was well established in ancient Greece and Rome, but many of the modern equestrian sports such as show jumping, dressage, horse trials, and long distance or cross-country riding, in fact have their origins in military practice.

In the 19th century, the armies of France, Germany, Sweden, and the U.S.A. staged 'endurance rides' as part of their cavalry training: rides varied from 18.5 miles to a staggering 350 miles, but no jumping was included: the emphasis was on stamina.

The French developed a more comprehensive test, the *Championnat du Cheval d'Armes* in 1902. A military exercise around Paris, the Championnat comprised a 'dressage' test, a steeplechase, a 30 mile race over road and track, and, a jumping competition. This formed the basis for the Three Day Event for military riders, which was included in the Olympic Games in 1912. Post-World War II, civilian riders began to participate, and the sport grew and gained impetus from the establishment in Britain of the Badminton Horse Trials, first staged in 1949.

ANDALUCIAN – GRAY.

109

THE CLASSIC AMERICAN SADDLEBRED.

In Italy, Captain Frederic Caprilli (1868-1907) chief instructor at the cavalry school at Pinerolo recognized that the 'knee-to-knee' charge of mounted squadrons in lines was no longer viable in warfare which now was increasingly dominated by firearms. Instead, Caprilli believed that the role of the cavalry was now to carry out aggressive reconnaissance missions which required riding across country swiftly, able to tackle any obstacles that lay in their path. To this end, Caprilli began training horses and riders to work with shortened stirrups, and to sit well forward in order that the rider's weight was carried as far over the horse's advancing center of balance as possible, where it would allow free movement of the horse. The basis of Caprilli's system – *il systema* – was adopted by cavalry schools across the world, and riders continue to 'sit forward' over fences.

Dressage comes from the French word *dresser* ('to train'), and is used in the context of training riding and harness horses. Dressage has its roots in the Renaissance but reached it heights in the 18th century under the influence of François Rubichon de la Guerinière, the father of 'Classical Riding', who published his book *École de Cavalerie* in 1733 and

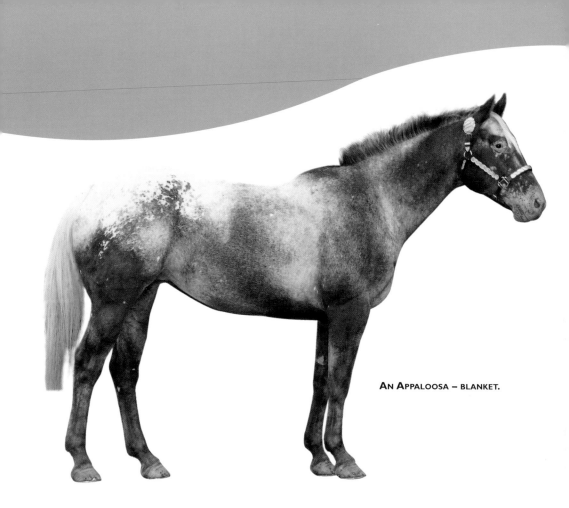

AN APPALOOSA – BLANKET.

whose principles are followed today. The cavalry instituted 'best trained charger' tests before dressage became a competitive sport with its first appearance at the Stockholm Olympics in 1912. Competitive dressage includes the very demanding Grand Prix test: advanced movements of passage, piaffe, canter, and pirouettes, as well as the precise execution of one-time changes at canter. The second leg of the contest, the Grand Prix Special, includes the Kur, the 'equine ballet', a freestyle competition set to music.

Out of a military background, horse riding would eventually develop into a highly sophisticated art form, and today the finest example is perhaps the beautiful Lipizzaner horses of the Spanish Riding School in Vienna (see page 186).

Cob

Height: Ideally, 15 hh (60 in.);
not exceeding 15.1 hh (61 in.)

Colors: All, but many are gray.

Use: Riding

Features: 'Workmanlike' head with an intelligent look; short, strong crested neck; strong, sloped shoulders; short, broad back; well-formed quarters; short powerful limbs; shot cannons, broad open feet.

Except for Welsh and Norman Cobs, the cob is a type of horse, not a recognized breed. It is a big-bodied, compact, utility horse that stands firmly and squarely on its short, powerful legs. In conformation, the cob is closer to the strong structure of a heavy horse rather than the longer limbed light horses which are designed for speed. A stocky but completely symmetrical horse at just about 15 hh

(60 in.), the cob is easy to mount and dismount and is expected to give a steady, dependable ride. In temperament the cob is endearingly referred to as a 'gentleman's gentlemen' (a butler) – calm, retiring, but very resourceful!

At one time it was the practice to dock the tails of cobs but this was deemed cruel and unnecessary in 1948 and was made illegal in the U.K. under the Docking and Nicking Act. Tails are now left full but the mane continues to be hogged, which does suit the neck shape of the cob. In the show ring, classes for cobs are divided into lightweight (capable of carrying up to 196 lb with 8 ½ inches of bone); heavyweight (capable of carrying over 196 lb and with at least 9 inches of bone), and working cobs, which are required to jump. In all classes, cobs must not exceed 15.1 hh (61 inches).

Arab

Height: **14.3–15 hh (57-60 in.)**
Colors: Gray, chestnut, bay, black
Use: Riding, improving other breeds
Features: Fine silky mane and tail which in
movement is carried arched and high; compact
body with short, slightly concave back; long level
croup; long, slender legs with short canons and
clearly defined tendons; head tapers to small
muzzle with large, flared nostrils and
magnificent, large, expressive eyes.

The debt owed by modern horse breeds to the Arabian, or Arab, cannot be underestimated: the Lipizzaner, the Akhal-Teke, the Thoroughbred, the Orlov Trotter, to name just a few have all been marked by Arab blood. The Arab is recognized as one of the 'fountainheads' of the world's horse breeds and because of its purity, it continues to act as an 'improver' – upgrading and refining other breeds.

It is claimed that the Arab was in existence at the time of the Prophet Muhammad and that it flourished at the courts of the Hashemite Princes in the 7th century. But it is possible that for more than 2,500 years, the Bedouin of Arabia had been breeding these prized horses. The Bedu kept few if any written records, but an oral tradition preserved the horses' pedigrees and maintains that the founding horses were the stallion, Hoshaba, and the mare Baz, who was captured in the Yemen by Bax, the great-great-grandson of Noah.

In AD 786, the historian El Kelbi, wrote the first 'history' and pedigree. Later, in the 19th century, the Emir Abd-el-Kader (1808-

and the head. The outline is governed by the fact that it has a unique skeletal formation: it has 17 ribs, 5 lumbar bones and 16 tail vertebrae where other breeds have an 18–6–18 arrangement. The difference in conformation accounts for the shape of the Arab's back and quarters and the beautiful high carriage of the tail. The head is very short and fine, with clearly visible veining. In profile it is noticeably dished or concave, while the forehead is convex and forms a shield shape bulge between the eyes called the jibbah, which extends from the ears to the nasal bone. A further distinguishing feature is the mitbah, the point where the head joins the neck: the greater the arch here, the greater the degree of mobility in the head in all directions. Additionally, the breed has what has been described as a 'floating action' – as though the horse was moving on invisible springs! Its stamina is legendary: they can maintain a run for over 100 miles, and while they can be over 60 inches (15 hh), on average, the Arab is around 57 inches (14.3 hh). Regardless of size, the magnificent Arab is always referred to as a horse – never a pony!

83) divided the Arab's history into four eras: from Adam to Ishmael (the outcast son of Abraham and the ancestor of the Bedu tribes); Ishmael to King Solomon (who, in spite of the Israelites' law forbidding keeping horses on the grounds of idolatry, kept 1,200 riding horses and 40,000 chariot horses in the royal stables!); Solomon to the Prophet Muhammad; and from the Prophet onwards. The spread of Islam also ensured the spread of the Arab throughout much of the Old World: it was introduced to Europe by the Moors who invaded Spain in the 7th century, and was instantly desired for its qualities of endurance, courage, gentleness, and great beauty. The Emperor Napoleon's horse, Marengo, which was ridden into battle at Waterloo, was a gray Arab.

The appearance of the Arab is unique: the most distinctive features are the outline

Egyptian Arabian

Evidence suggests that the Arab horse was being bred some 2,500 years ago on the Arabian peninsula where it was maintained in its pure form by Bedouin breeders. It was with the Muslim conquests of the 7th century AD that the breed's influence began to spread wider afield: by AD 700, the armies of Islam had conquered and occupied all of modern Turkey, Persia (modern Iran), Palestine, Syria, and North Africa including Libya, Morocco and Northern Egypt. From North Africa, the Moors invaded Spain and so, apart from southern Russia, all the most famous horse-breeding areas in the ancient world were now in their power. The finest stallions and mares were returned to the capital of the Islamic world, Damascus in Syria, where through selective breeding, they were molded to form the modern Arabians.

The different strains of Arabians in existence today may raise some controversial points, but basically, a strain is a female line descended through the generations from a particular foundation

Height: 14.3–15 hh (57–60 in.)
Colors: Gray, chestnut, bay, black
Use: Riding, improving other breeds
Features: Fine silky mane and tail which in movement is carried arched and high; compact body with short, slightly concave back; long level croup; long, slender legs with short canons and clearly defined tendons; head tapers to small muzzle with large, flared nostrils and magnificent, large, expressive eyes.

mare owned by a sheikh or a tribe. The dispersion of the Arab began many centuries ago: in 1350 the Rajput Sultan Allah-uh-Din gave 500 Arab horses as gifts on his son's marriage. The Mogul rulers of India, who brought with them the Persian tradition of owning horses of great beauty and size, were among the first to import Arabs sires with the aim of improving Indian breeds. The Egyptian influence is, however, one of the most important and most pervasive: the stud of Ali Pasha Sherif provided the stallions Mahruss II and Mesaoud that were returned to Lady Anne and Sir Wilfred Scawen Blunt's Crabbet stud in England in the late 19th century.

The modern Egyptian Arabs are derived from the herds of Mohammed Ali Pasha and his grandson, Abbas Pasha I, as well as 20 horses from Crabbet which were sent to Lady Blunt's Sheikh Obyed Stud in Egypt. The famous stallion Nazeer passed on his qualities to three sons: Ibn, Halima and Morafic, who went to the United States, while the third son, Aswan, was gifted by President Nasser of Egypt to the Tersk Stud in Russia.

Shagya Arabian

For more than 1,000 years, Hungary has been producing outstanding horses: the climate, and quality vegetation ensured strong animals. Hungarian horses were so highly prized that some 900 years ago, King Laszlo banned further exports from the country to preserve the native stock. Hungary's position at the 'crossroads of Europe' also made it subject to successive invasions and during a century and a half of occupation by the Turkish Ottoman Empire, the horse population was greatly influenced by Arab and Syrian stallions of the Ottoman cavalry.

Height: **15 hh (60 in.)**
Colors: **Often gray, but all solid colors can be found.**
Use: **Riding and harness work.**
Features: **Arab-type physique, but bigger with more substance and bone than many modern Arabs. Pronounced withers, a more sloping shoulder and notably correct hind legs.**

Two Hungarian breeds are derived from pure Arab: the Shagya Arab and the Gidran Arab. The Gidran Arab originated at Mezohegyes, the first modern stud in Hungary, founded in 1784. This, the oldest of the great Hungarian studs is also famed for the development of the Nonius (page 197) and Furioso breeds (page 162). The Shagya Arab originated at Babolna, northwestern Hungary, a stud founded in 1789, and now the headquarters of pure-bred Arabs in Hungary. The founding sire of the breed was the stallion Shagya, an Arab of the Kehilan/Siglavy strain, who was born in Syria in 1830 and brought to Babolna in 1836 along with seven other stallions and five mares. For an Arab horse, Shagya was large, standing 15.2 hh (62 in.) and was said to be a distinctive — and unusual — cream color. Shagya sired a number of very successful sons who ensured the continuation of the dynasty and his descendants can now be found at stud in Babolna as well as at stud in the Czech Republic, Austria, Poland, Germany, Russia, and Slovakia.

The Shagya Arab displays all the characteristics of the pure Arab — the good nature, good looks, and great intelligence — but rarely stands less than 15 hh (60 in.), and displays more bone and considerably more substance than pure-breds. The Shagya Arab, once a favorite mount of the Hungarian Hussars, is a very practical horse, used under saddle and in harness.

Polish Arabian

Height: **14.3–15 hh (57-60 in.)**
Colors: **Gray, chestnut, bay, black**
Use: **Riding, improving other breeds**
Features: **Arab-type physique**

Poland has been a country famous for horse breeding for many centuries, and eastern stallions of all varieties were captured from the Turks during a long series of wars. They undoubtedly had an effect on Polish horses and once a few pure-bred Arabian mares were captured, Arabians were bred pure in Poland. When the Turkish Wars ended at the beginning of the 18th century, Polish envoys were sent to Asia Minor to purchase stallions from Aleppo, Baghdad, and Damascus. In 1845, three pure-bred Arabian mares were imported to the Jarczowce Stud: these three mares were to establish the female line that flourishes today.

Since then, Poland has produced some of the finest Arabian horses in the world, and stallions have been in great demand worldwide: in 1912 the gray stallion Skowronek was exported to Britain where in 1920, he arrived at the Crabbet Stud. His descendants are still prominent in Britain, as well as in South America, Spain, the U.S.A., and in the former Soviet Union. In 1926 the Polish Arab Stud Book was introduced under the auspices of the Ministry of Agriculture. Previously, pedigrees had been kept by every stud. Many Polish Arabians have pedigrees that can be traced back for ten generations, and often, many more, extending over periods of 150-200 years. Janow Podlaski, founded in 1817, is now the main Polish stud where both pure-bred Arabs and Anglo-Arabs are produced today.

Anglo-Arab

Height: 16–16.3 hh (60-65 in.)

Colors: All solid colors

Use: Riding, racing, competition

Features: A tough, athletic horse with an outline that tends towards the Thoroughbred, with a straight head profile, well sloped shoulders, and prominent withers. The frame is more solid than a Thoroughbred and the croup is longer. Great jumping ability and well suited to dressage.

In England, Anglo-Arab is a cross between a Thoroughbred stallion, the world's greatest racehorse, and an Arab mare – or vice versa – with subsequent re-crossings. There are only two strains in the pedigree and to gain entry into the British stud book, a horse must be able to claim a minimum of 12.5% Arab blood. While the Anglo-Arab originated in Britain, it has also been bred extensively in France. for more than 150 years, where entry into the stud book requires a minimum of 25% Arab blood.

Ideally, the Anglo-Arab should have the Arab's qualities of soundness, endurance, and stamina, along with the size and some of the speed of the Thoroughbred – but without the latter's excitable manner. In Britain the popular breeding practice is to use an Arab stallion on a Thoroughbred mare when the offspring are likely to exceed either of the parents in size. (A Thoroughbred stallion on an Arab mare is considered to produce smaller offspring which are less valuable than pure-breds of either breed.)

In France, the principal breeding centers today are the studs at Pau, Pompadour, Tarbes and Gelos. French breeds owes much to the support given by the long established royal – then later, national – studs which were first created by Louis XIV in the 17th century. The systematic breeding of the Anglo-Arab began in 1836 based on two Arab stallions, Massoud and Aslan, and three Thoroughbred mares, Dair, Common Mare, and Selim Mare. A rigorous system of selection based on stamina, performance, and conformation was designed into the breeding program which continues to this day, with the later addition of a racing program confined to, and designed, to test the breed.

In appearance, the Anglo-Arab tends more towards the Thoroughbred than the Arab: the head is straight (rather than a concave profile), the neck is longer (indicative of greater speeds), the withers are more prominent, and the shoulders more oblique and powerful. The quarters have a tendency to be long and horizontal, but the frame is more 'solid' than a Thoroughbred's. The Anglo's feet are exceptionally sound and strong, and are rarely prone to disease. While the Anglo-Arab may not have the speed of the Thoroughbred, they are very agile and athletic horses: the Anglo-Arabs bred at Pompadour in France are noted not only for their size but also for their excellent jumping abilities.

Thoroughbred

Height: **Up to 16.1hh (64.5 in.)**
Colors: All solid colors
Use: Riding, especially racing, cross-breeding
Features: Fine, elegant head on long, arched neck; sloping shoulders and powerful hindquarters; deep chest to allow for maximum lung expansion; large, flat joints, strong legs with plenty of bone.

The Thoroughbred is the fastest and possibly, the most valuable horse in the world, as well as one of the most beautiful: perfectly proportioned and with enormous physical stamina, it is the quintessential racehorse. The Thoroughbred evolved in Britain in the 17th and 18th centuries to satisfy the enthusiasm of the English monarchs – and their subjects – for horse racing. Britain had long produced 'running horses' like the swift Galloways (the ancestors of the Fell Pony, see page 64), and the Irish Hobby (the forerunner of the Connemara, see page 54). King Henry VIII, the first royal patron of horse racing established the Royal Paddocks at Hampton Court and crossed native 'running horses' with horses from Spain and Italy – which were no doubt influenced by the Barb. Later monarchs also continued to maintain a strong interest in 'running horses'. In the 17th and 18th centuries, eastern breeds

were introduced – not for their speed, since there was little increase in comparison to the English 'running horses', but in order to breed true to type.

The Thoroughbred has three great founding Arab stallions – none of whom ever raced! The Byerly Turk took part in the Battle of the Boyne in 1690 before standing at stud in County Durham and founding the first of the principle bloodlines which began with Herod (foaled in 1758, the son of Jigg, by the Byerly Turk.)

The Darley Arab, standing at 60 in. (15 hh) was found at Aleppo in Syria in 1704 and sent to the owner's home in East Yorkshire. He was mated with the mare Betty Leedes and produced the first great racehorse, Flying Childers. His full brother,

Bartlett's Childers was the ancestor of Eclipse, who founded the second bloodline and some of the most influential bloodlines of the 20th century stem from him.

The Godolphin Arabian came to England in 1728 to Lord Godolphin's Gog Magog stud in Cambridgeshire and sired the mare Roxanna and produced Lath and Cade, who in turn sired Matchem in 1748 who leads the third line. A fourth bloodline was that of Highflyer, son of Herod. Most – 81% – of Thoroughbred genes are derived from 31 original ancestors, of whom the most important are the three founding stallions from whom all modern Thoroughbreds descend in the male line.

The modern Thoroughbred is bred to mature at an early age, with horses raced at two years old. The action is long and low: the hind leg from hip to hock is so long that the hind legs can achieve maximum thrust when galloping, while the depth of the girth also allows for maximum lung expansion, both essential features in a racehorse. The clean and very fine head of the Thoroughbred, with a covering of thin skin – thin enough to see the veins beneath – has a straight profile unlike its Arab ancestors. The eyes are large and alert, the ears mobile, the nostrils large. The Thoroughbred refinement also extends to the coat which is thin and silky. The principal colors of the breed are brown, bay, chestnut and black. Gray Thoroughbreds are a color attributed to the 17th century Alcock Arabian and Brownlow's Turk.

Akhal-Teke

Height: 15.2 hh (61 in.)

Colors: Chestnut, black, gray, 'golden-metallic' dun

Use: Riding, endurance, racing, competition

Features: Long, thin neck set high and almost vertical to the body; head joins neck at 45 degree angle; line from mouth is often higher than the withers – a feature peculiar to the breed. Coat is exceptionally fine and skin is thin; short, silky tail and sparse forelock and mane. Hard, small feet.

One of the most distinctive and unusual horses in the world, the Akhal-Teke is also one of the oldest breeds and is famous for its stamina and courage. The Akhal-Teke is a descendant of the Tarpan and Horse Type 3: horse skeletons excavated at Anau, near Ashkhabad, the capital city of the Republic of Turkmenistan in Central Asia, show that 'desert horses' – horses of fine bone and skin – were being bred in this region some 2,500 years ago.

In the later Middle Ages and Renaissance, Akhal-Teke horses were exported to Russia and other European centers where they were used extensively at stud: the Kuban Cossacks were often mounted on Akhal-Tekes. The breed is unique not only for its antiquity, but for the methods of horse breeding traditionally used in the oases of the Central Asian deserts. Throughout the year the Turkmeni kept their horses tethered and under blankets, and fed them with a light but highly nutritious mix of food including pellets of mutton fat, barley, eggs, and alfalfa as well as quatlame, a fried dough cake. The Akhal-

Teke became well suited to the hot environment and is capable of covering great distances in the harshest environments. In 1935, a group of Turkmeni riding Akhal-Teke and Jomud horses rode 2,580 miles from Ashkhabad to Moscow in 84 days. It became a historic venture, as it included a three-day journey with very little water, across 225 miles of the arid Kari-Kum Desert.

Today, the main breeding center remains the stud at Ashkhabad. The Akhal-Teke is a very distinctive, wiry, horse: by western standards it is not perfect, but this is recognized in the breed description. The body is long and narrow, the rib cage shallow, and often lacks the 'second thigh' prized by western riders. The hind legs are often sickle-shaped and cow-hocked, while the forelegs are usually set 'too close'

together. The mane and tail are sparse and fine in texture. A peculiar feature of the breed is for the head to be carried above the level of the rider's hands – a position called 'above the bit', which in the west is a position deemed to reduce the rider's control of the horse.

Nevertheless, the Akhal-Teke is a highly prized horse capable of great speed, of astonishing jumping, and with great qualities of endurance, as well as beauty and grace in movement. The action, like the breed itself, is unique: the Akhal-Teke is described as 'sliding' over the ground in a flowing movement without any swinging of the body. The colors of the fine coat can be chestnut, black, and, gray, but the most striking color is the dun, which has a gold or silver metallic sheen to it – especially when the horse stands in sunlight.

American Saddlebred

Height: 15–16 hh (60-64 in.)

Colors: Chestnut, bay, brown, and black. Palominos, grays and roans also appear.

Use: Riding and harness work, pleasure riding

Features: Small, elegant head set high on long, muscular neck; strong back, shoulders, and quarters; except when shown in harness, the feet are grown unnaturally long to enhance action and are shod with heavy shoes. Custom dictates tail is set high by nicking.

A handsome and showy horse with an elevated action, the American Saddlebred was originally known as the Kentucky Saddler, and was developed as an all-round horse for farm work, for riding, and for carriage work, by Kentucky plantation owners in the 19th century. The trotting horses, and the once highly prized ambling and pacing horses, went out of fashion in England in the 17th century when Thoroughbred (see page 122) racing became established, and many of these strains found their way to America where, in a short space of time, they founded the

'American breeds' in which the different gaits were preserved and refined. The American Saddlebred is based on two such gaited breeds: the Canadian Pacer and the Narragansett Pacer (both breeds are now extinct) with the added infusion of Morgan (see page 195) and Thoroughbred blood in order to produce this very impressive, speedy and elegant breed.

The modern Saddlebred is either three-gaited or five-gaited: a three-gaited Saddlebred performs at walk, trot, and, canter with each gait performed with a slow but high action. Three-gaited Saddlebreds are shown with a hogged mane and trimmed tail. The five-gaited Saddlebred has two extra paces: the 'slow gait', which is a four beat prancing movement, and the full speed 'rack', a high, four-beat gait free of any lateral movement or pacing action, which can achieve speeds of up to 38 mph. The five-gaited Saddlebred is shown with a full mane and tail. It is also an exceptional performer in harness: in show classes, they are judged on the quality of their walk and the spectacular controlled 'park walk'. With its feet normally trimmed – rather than left long for the show ring – the American Saddlebred is also used widely for pleasure and trail riding, as well as being used to cut cattle.

American Standardbred

Height: 15.2-16 hh (61-64 in.)

Colors: All solid colors

Use: Racing, driving

Features: A plain head, strong shoulders and perfect relationship to the neck; withers are well defined but may be lower than the croup; longer and lower body than a Thoroughbred, but powerful and deep in the girth; exceptionally powerful quarters; hind legs and hocks must be entirely correct in their construction; sound feet and perfectly straight action are required.

The American Standardbred is undoubtedly the most famous and the fastest trotter in the world and the finest proponent of a style of harness racing which is popular not only in the U.S.A., but in Europe, Russia, and Scandinavia. The term 'Standardbred' was first used in 1879 and it refers to the speed standard required for entry into the breed register. Originally the standard was set at three minutes, but later separate harness races were held for conventional, and for diagonal trotters and for pacers employing a lateral gait. The standard was then set at two minutes and 30 seconds for conventional trotters over a mile and two minutes 25 seconds for pacers over a mile. Today speeds of under two minutes are quite common. The pacer, which is faster and less likely to break the gait, is the preferred horse in the U.S.A., while in Europe, trotters are the more numerous.

The American Standardbred was first established in the eastern states of the U.S.A. in the late 18th century. It was founded on an English Thoroughbred called Messenger (a descendent of the Darley Arabian) who was imported from England in 1788. Although Messenger did not race in harness, like all early Thoroughbreds, he had trotting connections via the Norfolk Roadster. Messenger spent 20 years at stud in Pennsylvania, New York and New Jersey, where he was bred to Morgan (see page 195), Canadian and Narragansett Pacers. The foundation sire of the Standardbred was Messenger's inbred descendent, Hambletonian 10, foaled in 1849. He, too, never raced in harness, but he did have a peculiarity of conformation that would contribute to his success as a sire of harness racers. Hambletonian

measured 15.325 hh at the croup and 15.125 hh at the withers – a physique that gave enormous propulsive thrust to the quarters. Hambletonian 10 proved himself an equally prolific sire with no fewer than 1,335 offspring between 1851 and 1875.

Standardbred harness racers in the U.S.A. compete at over 70 major tracks. Racing is done at the lateral pacing gait with hobbles worn to prevent the gait being broken.

129

Andalucian

Height: 15.2 hh (61 in.)

Colors: Usually bay and shades of gray as well as a very striking mulberry shade

Use: Riding

Features: Hawk-like profile; long, often wavy mane and tail; strong quarters with high degree of articulation makes the breed well suited to the advanced movements of the menage; action described as 'proud' and 'lofty' with a slow, showy, rhythmical walk, a high-stepping trot, and a smooth rocking canter.

In the development of modern horse breeds, the Barb, the Arab and the Spanish horse, play a vital part. The Spanish horse has over the centuries been given a variety of names, most of which derive from the geographical areas in which they were bred: the Andalucian, the Carthusian, the Alter-Real, and the Peninsular. Some maintain that it would be better to know all these 'breeds' simply as the 'Iberian horse', which would then encompass near neighbors such as the Lusitano from Portugal. The Andalucian breed traces back to at least the time of the Moorish occupation of Spain, when Barb horses from North Africa were introduced to the Iberian peninsula. The mingling of Barb blood with native stock – local Sorraira ponies and descendants of the Vandal invasion tribe's tough Germanic horses brought to Spain in AD 405 – was to produce one of the foremost horses of Europe. The Andalucian's 'hawk-like' head owes much to the Barb. In turn, the Andalucian would influence many other European breeds including the Lipizzaner (see page 186), and American breeds such as the Paso Fino and Peruvian Paso (see page 211).

The name Andalucian is also vague: the region encompasses an area in southern Spain around Seville, Cordoba, and Granada, but for centuries, Andalus, in fact meant the whole of the southern Spanish peninsula. While many countries still use the appellation Andalucian, since 1912 Spanish breeders have known these horses as *Pura Raza Espanol* ('Pure Spanish Breed'). The center for breeding Andalucian horses today remains centered on Cordoba and Seville, and in the Carthusian monastery of Jerez de la Frontera founded in 1476, where for centuries, the monks maintained the purity of the breed by refusing to out-cross with heavy Neapolitan horses in spite of a royal edict which encouraged this practice.

The beautiful and commanding Andalucian has a showy and rhythmical walk, a high-steeping trot, and a smooth, spectacular rocking canter. While not a 'fast' horse, the Andalucian is enormously strong. The innate balance, and agility – coupled with the Andalucian's

courageous spirit and spectacular paces – make it well suited to both Haute École and to the bull ring, where it can be seen today. The usual colors of the Andalucian are bay and gray, but there were also strains in the 'old Spanish Horse' that were spotted and parti-colored: the coat patterns of the American Appaloosa and Pinto are inherited from Spanish horses taken to the New World by the Conquistadors in the 16th century. A most distinctive feature of the Andalucian is the long, luxuriant, and frequently wavy mane and tail.

Lusitano

Height: 15–16 hh (60-64 in.)

Colors: Predominantly gray, bay and the striking mulberry shade also occurring.

Use: Riding and harness work

Features: Head is straight or somewhat convex in profile; small alert ears; widely spaced eyes; short, thick neck; enormously powerful shoulders and quarters; short back and deep chest; long slender legs; full wavy tail and mane; naturally high action.

The Lusitano is the Portuguese 'blood-brother' of the Andalucian (see page 130): a handsome, compact, and high-stepping horse that takes its name from Lusitania, the Roman name for Portugal, and by which it has been officially known only since 1966. The precise origins of the breed are uncertain, but we do know that the Lusitano and Andalucian share the same genetic background and character, despite the significant differences in conformation. The Lusitano's croup is generally more sloped, the tail set lower, and the convexity in the head is more pronounced, but in both breeds, all shades of bay and gray, as well as the beautiful mulberry shade, are found.

The Lusitano has been bred since the 16th century in Portugal as the 'all-round' work horse: it was used for light agricultural work, as a carriage horse, and, as a cavalry mount. The breeding of Lusitanos is, however, most closely bound to the rearing and fighting of the famous black bulls of Portugal: the agile, intelligent, and fearless Lusitano is the

favored mount of the *campinos* who tend the herds, and of the *rejoneadores*, the mounted bullfighters. The entire bull fight — which is regarded as an art form in Portugal and the rules of which were laid down in the 18th century by the Marquis de Marialva (1713-99) — is carried out on horseback: the bull is not killed in the ring, and it is considered a great disgrace for a horse to be injured in any way. In the bull ring, the Lusitano displays its natural high-stepping action alongside the full range of dressage movements — which it performs at considerable speed. Consequently, this highly intelligent and very agile breed is beginning to attract a great deal of attention outside its native Portugal, especially in the U.S.A. and the U.K.

Appaloosa

Height: 14.2–15.2 hh (57-61 in.)

Colors: Spotted – in five basic patterns – usually gray on roan

Use: Riding – including rodeo

Features: Skin on nose, lips and genitals is mottled; sclera (membrane around iris of eye) is white; feet often vertically striped; tail and mane are sparse.

The Appaloosa is an American spotted breed developed by the Nez Perce Indians in the Palouse Valley (Appaloosa is a corruption of Palouse) in northeast Oregon in the 18th century. The Nez Perce excelled at horse breeding and developed animals of such high quality that the merits of their horses were singled out in the journal of Meriwether Lewis, in the Lewis and Clarke expedition to Oregon in 1806.

In October 1877, the Nez Perce were wiped out in a battle with the U.S. Army which lasted for six days, but the legacy of the tribe in the form of the Appaloosa lived on: in 1938 the breed was revived under the auspices of the Appaloosa Horse Club, founded in Moscow, Iowa, and the breed is today one of the most popular in the United States, with over 65,000 registrations – the third largest breed registry in the world!

Spotted horses have however been around for thousands of years and the Appaloosa's coat is the result of a hereditary gene whereby can appear with any other solid body color, roan being the most common. Spotted horses probably arrived in North America with the Spaniards in the 16th century, and some of the horses undoubtedly carried the spotting gene and found their way to the northeastern states of the U.S.A. Other spotted American horses include the Pony of the Americas, a 'breed' developed from an Appaloosa/Shetland cross, and, the Colorado Ranger Horse (see page 146) based on Arab and Barb foundations.

Unlike the Pinto's broad blotches and randomly shaped forms and shapes which mark its coat (see page 205), the Appaloosa's spots usually assume an organised pattern in which the designs are regular and remarkably precise. There are five basic patterns of spotting in the Appaloosa: leopard, an all-over spotted pattern of dark 'egg-shaped' spots on a white background; snowflake, which consists of light spots on a dark background; blanket, where the coat color over the hips can be white (white blanket) or when spots occur only on the loins and hindquarters (spotted blanket); marble, which is a mottling all over the body; and, frost, a white speckling on a dark

background. The usual ground color of the Appaloosa is roan; the skin around the nose, lips, and genitals is mottled, and the sclera — the membrane around the iris of the eye — is white. Furthermore, the feet are often distinguished by vertical black and white stripes, while the mane and tail are notable sparse and wispy. It is said the Nez Perce encouraged this so the hairs didn't get caught up in the thorny shrub they rode through. The modern Appaloosa stands between 14.2–15.2 hh (57-61 in.): while the Nez Perce needed practical, sturdy horses that were suitable for hunting and for defence, today, the Appaloosa is used primarily as a stock and pleasure horse, as well as for racing, jumping, western, and long-distance riding.

Azteca

Height: 14.2–16 hh (57-60 in.)

Colors: All solid colors, and Tobiano and Overo markings

Use: Riding, trail riding, ranch work

Features: Medium-sized head with straight profile (although it can be either slightly convex or concave); broad forehead; slightly arched well-muscled neck; long, sloping shoulders; long flowing tail and mane; knee action can be high and brilliant, or, long and flowing .

The Azteca is often called the 'National Horse of Mexico' and is a recent breed innovation. In 1972, the *Charros* – the Mexican cowboys – set out to produce a horse with the speed, stamina, agility and 'cow sense' needed to work their ranches. Crossing the Andalucian (see page 130) with their Quarter Horses (see page 213) and Criollo mares (see page 148) they produced an outstandingly versatile and beautiful horse, the Azteca. The Andalucian – the 'Spanish Horse' – gave the new breed its sloping shoulders, sturdy legs and hooves, and its stamina, as well as its high stepping action and luxuriant mane and tail. The Andalucian was once the foremost horse of Europe: they were so highly prized that Napoleon stole nearly all of them from Spain during his campaign in the Peninsula War of 1808! Today, the Andalucian, like the Azteca, also works with cattle – but often in the bullrings of Spain. Today, more than three-quarters of all modern breeds – including the Quarter Horse – trace their origins back to the 'Spanish Horse'.

It is from the Quarter Horse that the Azteca gains its strength and speed: the Quarter Horse, developed by the early English colonists in the Virginias and Carolinas, got its name from the three-quarter mile sprints at which it excelled. Azteca breed requirements mean that the Azteca should have no more than three-quarters Andalucian or Quarter Horse blood in the first generations. The aim is for a 'blood balance' between breeds to encourage the best qualities of both. Both Quarter Horses and Paint Horses (see page 205) are used for breeding Aztecas: consequently, all the solid colors of the Quarter Horse, and the Tobiano (a white base overlaid with large patches of solid color) and Overo (a solid coat color with irregular patches of white) markings of the Paint Horse are acceptable in the Azteca. They are also distinguished by their long flowing manes and tails, and the varied knee action produces both elevated and suspended gaits, as well as a long and flowing action. This makes the Azteca an ideal horse not only for cow cutting but for haute école as well.

Bavarian Warmblood

Height: 15.2–16.2 hh (61–65 in.)
Colors: Chestnut, all solid colors
Use: Riding, carriage, light draft
Features: Strong legs; very sound feet; deep girth, steady, reliable temperament; branded with a 'B' in a coat of arms surmounted by a stylized crown.

Although it is one of the less well known of the German Warmbloods, the Bavarian is one of the oldest, as its origins can be traced back to well before the Crusades. Its ancestor was the Rotaller, which originated in the fertile Rott Valley in Bavaria, a region famous for its horse breeding producing highly prized heavy military horses

Systematic breeding began in the 16th century at the monastic studs of Hornbach and Worschweiler in the Zweibrucken region, and in the 18th century the stock was further improved by the introduction of half-bred English stallions, Cleveland Bays

and Norman Cobs. By the end of the 19th century, Oldenburgers were introduced to give the Rotallers more substance in response to demand for heavily built warmbloods. Thoroughbred blood was also introduced which made the Rotaller a lighter, though still very strongly built horse, about 16 hh (1.63m), well-proportioned and with good bone.

In the 1960s, the traditional name of Rotaller was discontinued, and the modern name of Bavarian Warmblood introduced. In spite of the name change, the Bavarian maintains the Rotaller's traditional chestnut coloring. Breeders today concentrate on producing these splendid horses with a quiet temperament: all Bavarians undergo performance testing. As a breed they are well suited to dressage and jumping, but like many other warmbloods, they are not the greatest of gallopers.

Belgian Warmblood

Height: 15.2–16.2 hh (61–65 in.)
Colors: All solid colors
Use: Riding, jumping
Features: Short, strong neck; deep and wide chest; solid, short limbs with good bones and feet; well rounded body; powerful, sloping quarters; high set tail.

For centuries Belgium has been famous for breeding massive heavy horses such as the Brabant and Ardennes, but more recently, in an effort to meet the demand for competition riding horses, the emphasis has shifted to breeding warmbloods. The Belgian Warmblood is a recent member of the European warmblood family and in a relatively short time, has shown itself to be a breed that excels at competition dressage and show jumping. The Belgian Warmblood, which has an average foal crop of some 4,500 per year is bred all over Belgium, especially in the traditional horse-breeding region of Brabant.

The history of the Belgian Warmblood begins in the 1950s when the lighter and cleaner legged Belgian farm horses were crossed first with Gelderlanders, then later with Holsteiner stallions and the athletic Selle Français – both of which have Thoroughbred backgrounds and are renowned for their straight, rhythmic action. In order to produce the finest possible competition horse, pure Thoroughbred blood was introduced, while to fix the temperament, Anglo-Arab and Dutch Warmblood crosses were added.

The Belgian Warmblood is a powerful, agile and calm horse that is now purpose bred for both dressage and jumping: strong loins, coupled with a short, elevated stride give it a natural advantage.

Budenny/Budyonny

Height: Average 16 hh (64 in.)

Colors: All solid colors, but 80% are chestnut.

Use: Originally a cavalry mount, today used in competitive riding: eventing, dressage and long distance events.

Features: Lightly built, but with comparatively heavy body; long straight neck; 'dry' head, veins show through the fine supple skin; the limbs are not the best, but the breed is nevertheless, incredibly tough.

The Budenny, or Budyonny, is one of the breeds developed in the early 20th century in the Soviet Union. The Budenny is named after the Bolshevik cavalry general, Marshal Budenny, a commander in the Russian Civil War (1918-20) and who initiated a breeding program in the Rostov region on the shores of the Black Sea in the 1920s. This later became the Budenny and First Cavalry Army Studs. The marshall began his program by crossing selected Don (see page 153) and Chernomor mares with Thoroughbred stallions (see page 122) to produce 'Anglo-Dons' – in essence, a 'Russian Warmblood'. The Chernomor is a Cossack horse very similar to the Don, but smaller, lighter, and more active, which was bred originally around Krasnodar, to the north of the Caucasus Mountains.

In a complex crossbreeding program, the best of the offspring were interbred in order to produce a tough, resilient and strong foundation stock. Special care was taken with the brood mares which were entitled to the finest pastures and winter accommodation. From the beginning of the breeding program, the young stock aged between two and four years, were performance-tested on the racecourse and in cavalry trials. A total of 657 mares were used to create the fixed type: 359 were Anglo-Dons; 261 were

Anglo-Dons crossed with Chernomors, and 37 were Anglo-Chernomors. These mares were mated with Anglo-Don stallions, and subsequently, any mares lacking sufficient Thoroughbred character were put back to Thoroughbred stallions.

Although in 1949, the Budenny breed was officially recognized, in the early days three distinct types were recognized: 'Massive', 'Eastern', and 'Middle'. As demand for an all-purpose competition horse grew, the production of a single type with a greater proportion of Thoroughbred blood was encouraged. The modern

Budenny stands on average 16 hh (64 in.) and the average measurements for a stallion are (ideally): length of barrel: 5 ft 4 in.; girth: 6 ft 3 in.; and bone below the knee: 8 inches. This latter measure is described as 'optimistic' since the Budenny's limbs reflect the qualities of the base stock, rather than the Thoroughbred. Nevertheless, the Budenny is a very tough horse. Around 80% are chestnut – often with a beautiful golden sheen which also betrays their Don and Chernomor ancestry. Bay, brown and black horses are also found.

Carmargue

Height: 14–15 hh (56–60 in.)

Colors: Foals are born black, dark gray or brown, lightening to gray or white

Use: Riding

Features: Long, high-stepping walk but short trot; agile and sure-footed; short necks; usually upright shoulders; deep chest; strong and fairly short back; very hard feet which are rarely shod; overall impression is of a 'primitive' horse.

The Camargue area where these horses live is in southwestern France, in the Rhône delta between the town of Aigues-Mortes and the sea. This is a harsh region in both landscape and climate: fiercely hot in summer, the rest of the year, the area is covered in cold, salt water through which the icy mistral wind rips. As well as the color, the most striking thing about the Carmargue horses is that they thrive on a diet of salt water and tough grasses. Although it is only since 1968 that the Camargue has been recognized as a breed, the horses are indigenous to the region and have probably been in existence there since prehistoric times, as these white horses bear a striking resemblance to those painted in the caves at Lascaux and Niaux which date from c.15,000 BC.

Although a large area of the Camargue has been drained and given over to agriculture, *manades* (herds) still roam free across the lagoon of Étang de Vacares, a 17,000 acre (6,880 hectare) nature reserve where the sight of them galloping through the sea shallows has earned them the nickname of 'the horses of the sea'. They are rounded up annually, branded, and selective gelding takes place under the auspices of the Nîmes National Stud. The Camargue horses are also used in their traditional role as the mounts for the guardians, the French cowboys of the south who tend and herd the famous black cattle of the Rhône delta. The guardians use a horsehair lariat and a trident to work their cattle, and employ the deep-seated saddle with a high cantle and caged stirrups that is used throughout the Iberian Peninsula.

The joy of seeing the Camargue horses outweighs the fact that they do not, in fact, have a particularly good conformation: the heads are often coarse and heavy, the necks short, and the shoulders inclined to be upright. But to compensate, they are deep in the girth and have good, strong backs and very

tough feet which are seldom shod. The Camargues in short, are incredibly hardy horses with great stamina and an ability to survive on the most meagre of diets.

All foals are born black, dark gray, or brown, and lighten as they mature. This can be a slow process: the Camargue does not reach adulthood until it is between five and seven years old – but it is exceptionally long-lived, often exceeding 25 years. As well as its white coat, the Camargue is also distinguished by its very distinctive action: the walk is long and high-stepping, and it can twist and turn during a gallop. These are the paces at which the Camargue is worked largely because the horse's 'upright' shoulders make for short and stilted trotting action.

Cleveland Bay

Height: 16–16.2 hh (60–60 in.)
Colors: All are bay with black points
Use: Riding, driving, light draft work
Features: Large convex head; powerful in the neck and shoulders; bone below the knee often 9 in. or more; clean legs, without feathers; open feet with hard, dense horn, large, well-ribbed body; thick black mane and tail.

Apart from Britain's indigenous ponies, the Cleveland Bay is the U.K.'s oldest and purest breed, for it has only a touch of Andalucian and Barb blood that was added in the 17th century. The beautiful Cleveland Bay, one of the longest-lived and most fertile breeds, originated in the Middle Ages in Wapentake of Langbaurgh, an area that

today corresponds with northeast Yorkshire and Cleveland. It evolved from the bay-colored Chapman horse (or Vardy if it was bred north of the River Tees) that was used by 'chapmen', or travelling salesmen. The Chapman horse was also used to transport the region's mining products like ironstone, potash, and alum from the hill mines to river or sea ports. The Chapman was, however, a much smaller horse than the modern Cleveland, but even at around 14 hh (56 in.) it was immensely powerful: the Chapman was known to carry a 220 lb (200 cwt) load over some of the roughest land in Britain.

The proud boast of Cleveland breeders is that their stock has 'No taint of Black nor Blood' – that is, the horse is untouched by either cart horse or Thoroughbred introductions. Two early 'Thoroughbred' sires Jalep (the grandson of the Godolphin Arab) and Manica (a son of the Darley Arabian) do appear in the General Stud Book, but this was long before the Thoroughbred was recognized – and recognizable – in its present form. Of greater influence was the Andalucian (see page 130) and the Barb: in the 16th and 17th centuries there were a great number of these 'Spanish horses' in the northeast of

England, and, there was a great deal of traffic between the northeast seaports and the Barbary coast. The marriage of Catherine of Braganza to Charles II in 1661 brought the North African harbor of Tangiers to the British crown and the port constructed there was built by contractors from Yorkshire.

The Cleveland's head still betrays some of the characteristics of the Andalucian – although these are not as evident in the modern breed as they once were in the horses of the Renaissance. The sometimes convex profile – which in earlier times was called 'hawk-like' or 'ram-like' is typical of Spanish stock. After the 18th century, there is no evidence of any infusions of 'foreign' blood and so by then the Cleveland Bay was fixed in type.

Until the reign of George II (r.1727-60) the Cleveland Bay was considered the best and most powerful coach horse in Europe. But new road building technology brought about macadamised roads and the Cleveland was then deemed too slow to maintain the speeds the coaches now

required. Consequently, it became relegated largely to farm work since it was the only horse that could work the heavy clay in north Yorkshire. The Cleveland went into a steady decline and by 1962, there were only four pure-bred stallions in the country. The breed was saved by H M Queen Elizabeth II, who bought the stallion Mulgrave Supreme and began a breeding program. In 15 years, there were 36 pure-bred stallions in the U.K. The royal Cleveland Bays live in the Royal Mews behind Buckingham Palace in London, and can be seen drawing the royal carriages on ceremonial processions.

There is, however, a shortage of pure-bred mares, and the Cleveland Bay is currently classified as 'critical' by the Rare Breeds Survival Trust.

145

Colorado Ranger

Height: Average 15.2 hh (61 in.)

Colors: All Appaloosa colors and patterns
(see page 134)

Use: Riding and harness work

Features: Compact with powerful limbs and quarters; small head on strong neck; sound, hard, open feet; spotted coats.

Although the U.S.A. has an enormous range of horses and ponies with a wide variety of coat colors, there are only three spotted breeds: the Appaloosa (see page 134), the Pony of the Americas, and the colorful Colorado Ranger Horse. This breed takes its name from the U.S. state in which it was developed, but it did not originate there. In 1878 Ulysses S. Grant was on a visit to Constantinople (now modern Istanbul) to the Sultan Abdul Hamid of Turkey when he was presented with a gift of two horses: a gray, pure-bred Siglavy-Gidran Arab called Leopard, and a pure blue-gray Barb called Linden Tree. These two horses were taken to Virginia to the stud of Randolph Huntingdon, who proposed using them as the foundation sires for a breed he envisaged as the 'Americo-Arab'.

The two were then 'vacationed' for a season at the Colby Ranch in Nebraska where they sired stock from the native mares, some of which were spotted or colored, which could have been inherited from the Barb via the Spanish horses brought to the New World in the 16th century. These stunning horses soon attracted attention from Western breeders: A.C Whipple of Kit Carson County, Colorado purchased mares from the Colby ranch, along with a white stallion with black ears called Tony, who was 'double-bred' to Leopard. Consequently, Leopard became the grand sire on both sides of the pedigree and the Whipples continued to extensively line-breed using him and his sons.

But the modern Colorado Ranger breed is essentially the product of Mike Ruby of the Lazy Z Bar Ranch: he bought Patches (son of Tony) and then a Barb called Max who was the son of Waldron Leopard of the original line. Ruby used the two as the foundation sires for the new breed which was now displaying a wide range of unusual colors. In 1934, the breed was named the Colorado Ranger Horse with Ruby as the president of the Association until his death in 1942. The Colorado Rangers were bred as working horses: compact, yet tough and very strong, they have very sound, open feet as a result of hard ground surfaces. All Appaloosa colors and patterns are accepted in the Colorado Ranger: in fact, a Ranger can be registered as an Appaloosa, but an Appaloosa cannot be registered as a Ranger. This is because, entry to the Colorado Ranger Stud Book is governed not by color (although they must have a patterned coat), but by the possession of the pedigree which must be traceable back to the foundation bloodlines.

Criollo

Height: 14–15 hh (56-60 in.)

Colors: Classically dun with dark dorsal stripe, but roan, chestnut, bay, black, and gray also appear.

Use: Military mounts and pack horses; riding, ranch work, and as a polo pony.

Features: Convex head on elegant, muscular neck; long, sloping shoulders; short limbs with prominent joints and short cannon; strong, compact back and well-muscled loin; well developed second thigh; hard-wearing feet. Some Criollos retain the lateral ambling gait of their Spanish horse ancestry.

The Criollo comes from Argentina, where horses continue to play a major part in the economy: they provide transport in the remote mountain regions, and as petroleum has to be imported, mechanization in agriculture has been restricted. The horse plays an equally important role in Argentine culture, for when Criollos are crossed with Thoroughbreds, they provide the base for the finest polo ponies in the world.

'Criollo' means 'of Spanish descent' and the term covers a number of South American horses: in Brazil it is called the *Crioulo*, in Chile, the *Caballo Chileno*, in Venezuela it is called the *Llnarero*, while in Peru, there are three types: the *Costerno*, the *Morochuco*, and the *Chola*. The

Argentinean Criollo descends from early Andalucian (see page 130) stock in which Barb blood was pre-eminent. Additionally, there is Sorraia blood. The first significant introduction of horses to Argentina was made in 1535 by Pedro de Mendoza, the founder of Buenos Aires, who brought 100 horses to the Rio de la Plata. Five years later, when the settlement was sacked by the indigenous Charros Indians, the horses escaped and within 50 years had bred so freely that some herds were estimated at 20,000 strong!

Little known outside South America, the Criollo is the mount of the famous gauchos. Tough, sound, and capable of carrying the heaviest weights over great distances and the hardest of terrain, the Criollo is well suited to a severe climate, little food and an almost constant shortage of water. Only the hardiest of animals are capable of surviving these conditions. In 1918 a breed society was formed and instituted endurance tests as a means of selection: a 470 mile 'march' had to be covered in 15 days with a pack weighing 242 lb – without any extra feed! The most famous 'endurance test' made by Criollo horses was in 1925: Professor Aime

Tschiffely travelled with Mancha (aged 15 years) and Gato Cardell (aged 16) from Buenos Aires to Washington D.C: a distance of 10,000 miles in 2 ½ years over some of the most inhospitable country in the world, including the Condor Pass at a height of over 18,000 feet in sub-zero temperatures. Gato Cardell lived to be 34, and Mancha, to 37 – and it is claimed that neither had a day's illness in their lives!

The coat color of the stockily built Criollo is varied: chestnut, bay, black, and gray, as well as blue and strawberry roans, skewbald and piebald occur, but dun shades predominate, with the most prized color in the breed being *grullo* or *gateado*, a mousey brown-dun shade.

Danish Warmblood

Height: 16.1–16.2 hh (64–65 in.)
Colors: All solid colors, but bay is most common
Use: Riding, competition
Features: Thoroughbred influence evident in head; clean throat with no fleshiness in the jowls; powerful limbs with good, clean joints; short cannons and good bone below the knee; well placed withers merge with sloping riding shoulders; good quality, even feet.

The Danish Warmblood, formerly known as the Danish Sports Horse, is a recent breed with its Stud Book opened only in the 1960s. Early horse breeding in Denmark occurred at the Cistercian monastery at Holstein where the large German mares were crossed with Spanish stallions to produce horses like the Frederiksborg and the Holsteiner (see page 174).

The basis for the new Danish Warmblood was the old Frederiksborg stock crossed with the Thoroughbred. The half-bred mares were then put to Selle Français to improve conformation and introduce a more athletic character; to Wielkopolski (a Polish warmblood related the Trakehner) which improved stamina and helped to fix the type, and to Thoroughbreds, which gave the Danish horse a further refinement and improved movement, speed and courage. The resulting Danish Warmblood is a handsome horse of Thoroughbred type, but with the substance and strength of its Frederiksborg ancestry.

Standing at an average of 16.2 hh (65 in.) the modern Danish Warmblood is regarded as one of the finest European-bred competition horses, excelling at dressage and often at cross country events as well. Its limbs are powerful, the joints large and well defined, and there is ample bone to carry the combined weight of both horse and rider.

Dutch Warmblood

Since the 11th century, horse breeding in Europe was primarily the concern of the agricultural industry and was supported by the great royal and state studs, especially when war horses, cavalry mounts, and coach horses were required. By the end of the 19th century and the early 20th century, with increased mechanization in transport, agriculture, and warfare, these types of horses had had their heyday. In the 20th century, the emphasis shifted from heavier working horses to lighter riding horses more suited to sport and recreation.

The Dutch Warmblood is one such horse: first bred in the Netherlands in the early 1900s, it is the product of Holland's two indigenous breeds, the Gelderlander (see page 164), a carriage horse with a strong front, and the heavy, powerfully quartered Groningen. What Dutch breeders did was basically combine the front and back of these two breeds into one, and then adjust the progeny by out-crosses to Thoroughbreds. The result was a more refined horse that still maintained the best qualities of the original Dutch breeds but was improved by the introduction of Thoroughbred blood which also increased their speed, stamina and courage: the carriage horse action and the long, harness back were eliminated, while length was added to the once short, thick neck.

Height: Average 16 hh (64 in.) and above
Colors: All solid colors with bay and brown most common
Use: Riding, competition
Features: Thoroughbred-type head on strong neck and withers; short, strong back; strong shoulders and deep front; strong limbs with short cannons; good feet.

Dutch Warmbloods stallions undergo a strict selection process under the auspices of the Warmblood Paardenstamboed Nederland to ensure only horses of excellent conformation, character, and temperament are used in breeding. Tests include jumping, cross country trials and occasionally, harness work. More than 14,000 mares are mated each year, and these are also tested for conformation, action, and temperament.

Don

One of the best known of the Russian breeds, the Don is the horse of the famous Cossacks: when most of Napoleon's horses died during the harsh winter of the French retreat from Moscow in 1812, the tough Don endured. The breed evolved in the 18th and 19th centuries from the horses reared by the nomadic tribes on the pastures of the Don steppes. Early influences were undoubtedly the Mongolian Nagai, horses of northern Iran, Persian Arabs, the Turkmene, a desert horse closely

Height: 15.3–16.2 hh (61-65 in.)

Colors: Chestnut and brown, often with a golden sheen

Use: Riding, light agricultural work

Features: Medium head with straight profile; straight neck; short straight shoulders; well developed chest; rounded croup with quarters tending to slope away; hind legs have tendency to be sickle-hocked; forelegs are generally straight, but there is tendency to 'calf knees' – an inward curve below the knee; tail and mane usually short and thin.

153

related to the Akhal-Teke (see page 124), and the Karabakh, a horse from the mountains of Azerbaijan. The influence of these last two horses is evident in the golden sheen of the Don's chestnut or brown coat color. In the 19th century, Dons were improved by the Cossacks using Orlovs (see page 203), Thoroughbreds, and Anglo-Arabs, but from the beginning of the 20th century, the breed has been kept pure and no outside blood has been introduced.

The Don horses are never 'pampered' but instead, fend largely for themselves, in winter, feeding off frozen grass under snow which was cleared by scraping with their hooves. While not the most elegant equine, the Don is nonetheless tough and versatile, able to adapt to a range of climatic conditions with apparent ease. Famous for their endurance, the Don is an all-purpose horse worked under saddle and in harness, and is used by the shepherds of the steppes and in the semi-desert regions of Kazakhstan and Kirghizstan. Many Dons are today also bred in the Budenny (see page 140) and Zimovnikov Studs in the Rostov region of the Black Sea.

In spite of its rather restricted and stilted action caused by the straight, short shoulders, 'calf knees' (an inward curve below the knees), a tendency towards sickle-hocks and upright pasterns, the Don also excels at long distance races! A standard test under saddle is a ride of 170 miles) – to be covered in under 24 hours.

Swedish Warmblood

Height: 16.2 hh (65 in.)
Colors: All solid colors
Use: Riding, competition
Features: Strong and sound; compact body carried on short, strong legs; good bone and short cannons below large, flat knees.

The Swedish Warmblood – also known as the 'Half-Blood' in deference to the Thoroughbred blood used to refine and develop the breed – was first bred in the 17th century as a cavalry horse at the great studs at Stromsholm.

The Swedish Warmblood is based on a variety of imported horses: from neighboring Denmark, France, Germany, and England, as well as from Russia, Hungary, Spain, and Turkey. The result of such a 'cocktail' of influences meant that in the early days, there was no fixed type, but the Spanish and Friesian imports along with the oriental horses, when mated with local mares, produced very strong offspring. Arab, Thoroughbred, Hanoverian, and Trakehner blood was introduced in both the 19th century and again in the 1920s and 1930s and resulted in big and powerful horses that were more fixed in type.

The resulting modern Swedish Warmblood is a strong, sound, and very sensible riding horse with an easy temperament and straight paces. With Trakehner ancestry, it is not surprising that the Swedish Warmblood is an excellent dressage horse, as well as being good show jumpers and event horses. They are also highly regarded as driving horses. Before being accepted for breeding, individuals are subjected to rigorous performance and temperament testing to ensure the finest qualities which are embodied in the breed are maintained.

Florida Cracker

Height: 13.5–15.2 hh (54-61 in.)
Colors: Solid colors and grays predominate
Use: Riding, ranch work
Features: Refined head; gray, blue, or dark eyes with white sclera; well-defined, narrow neck without excessive crest; short, strong back, well-sprung rib cage; sloping croup and medium-set tail; natural ability to gait.

The Florida Cracker traces its origins back to the Spanish horses brought to the New World by the Conquistadors in the 16th century. Their mixed ancestry includes North African Barb, Spanish Sorraia, and Jennet, as well as Andalucian blood, which makes the Florida Cracker similar to the Spanish Mustang (see page 226), the Argentine Criollo (see page 148), and the Peruvian Paso and Paso Fino, which are also descendants of the horses introduced by the Spanish to the Caribbean Islands and the Americas. The Cracker was to become a distinct part of this breed family because of its isolation in Florida, where the herds roamed freely. Their natural herding instinct combined with their Spanish ancestry accounts for the Florida Cracker's naturally fast walk. While not all Crackers are considered as 'gaited', most do however perform a gait called the 'Coon Rack'.

Other gaits performed by the Cracker include the flatfoot walk, running walk, trot, and ambling or 'Paso-type' gait.

Because of its ability to survive in, and adapt to, its isolated environment, the Florida Cracker became an essential part of the state's cattle-based economy. Florida cowboys were nicknamed 'crackers' because of the sound made by their whips as they cracked in the air. This became the name given to both the cattle they tended, and eventually to the small, very agile horses they rode. The Florida Cracker has also been known as the Chickasaw Pony, Seminole Pony, March Tackie, Grass Gut, and Florida Cow Pony.

In the 1930s, however, the breed suffered

a reversal of fortune: the Great Depression led to a number of government-sponsored relief programs, and one of these was to encourage moving cattle from the Dust Bowl of the Midwest states to Florida. With these cattle came the screw worm parasite which was to change the practice of cattle raising. Before screw worm, cowboys were able to use the small, fleet-footed Crackers to herd and drive cattle. Screw worm-infected cattle required roping so they could be held for veterinary treatment and a larger and stronger horse like the Quarterhorse (see page 213) was needed for this task. As a result, the Cracker went into decline.

The Cracker is now rare (but lucky). There is an estimated population worldwide of just 2,000 or so horses with fewer than 100 new registrations each year. Nevertheless, the breed has survived, thanks to the efforts of a few dedicated families who kept the distinct bloodlines alive in their herds, and numbers are increasing slowly, but steadily.

These families include the Ayers, Harvey, Bronson, Partin, Matchetts, and Whaley families. Furthermore, in 1984 John Ayers donated a group of horses to the Florida State Department of Agriculture and Consumer Services to begin the Withlacoochee State Forest Cracker herd. This was followed by the purchase of further Crackers which were released on the Paynes Prairie State Preserve, and the establishment in 1989 of the Florida Cracker Horse Association which united owners and breeders in one organization. In 1991 the Florida Cracker Horse Registry began registering horses under strict guidelines in order to protect purity of the bloodlines: horses may be registered under the Foundation Series or the Cracker Series (the descendants of the Foundation horses).

French Trotter

Height: Average 16.2 hh (65 in.)
Colors: Black, brown, gray, and chestnut
Use: Trotting, both in harness and ridden
Features: Alert head on strong, straight neck; flat withers; strong trotting shoulders that are sufficiently sloped to give a long action; muscular quarters; long, hard legs with short cannons and strong feet.

Taller and more powerful than other trotters, the French Trotter, was developed in the 19th century in Normandy, France. Breeders who had produced tough, all-round foundation horses for breeding both riding and light draft military use, began to specialize in horses of both types. Supported by the Administration of National Studs, the French began importing English Thoroughbreds (see page 122), half-bred or Hunter stallions (see page 176) and the greatest trotting horse in Europe under saddle or in harness, the incomparable Norfolk Roadster. Two of the most important English horses to contribute to the breed were the half-bred Young Ratler – often called the 'French Messenger' because his influence on the French Trotter was comparable to that of Messenger, the foundation sire of the American Standardbred – and the Thoroughbred Heir

of the Linne. Ultimately, five important bloodlines were established to which most modern French Trotters can trace back: these lines were Conquerant, Lavater, Normand, Phaeton, and, Fuschia. Later American Standardbred blood was introduced to give the French Trotter more speed, but without loosing its larger size and diagonal trotting gait.

The sport of trotting, both in harness and under saddle was stabilized in the 19th century in France: the first trotting races for ridden horses were staged on the Champs de Mars in Paris in 1806 and the first purpose-built raceway was constructed at Cherbourg in 1836. Today, 10% of all French trotting races are for horses under saddle which has encouraged a more substantially built horse able to carry a relatively heavy weight that is level in its action.

The premier ridden race in France is the Prix de Cornulier; and the harness equivalent is the Prix d'Amerique, both staged at the Hippodrome de Vincennes. This track is considered the supreme test for both saddle and harness trotter: it begins downhill, then levels out until the last 1,000 yards of the 1 ¼ mile track when it turns steeply uphill. In 1989, the qualification time for entry in races for horses of four years old and over was 1 minute 22 seconds over ⅗ mile.

Recognized as a breed in 1922, the French Trotter has also contributed to the development of the Selle Français (see page 224) and is also noted as a sire of jumpers.

Friesian

Height: Average 15 hh (60 in.)
Colors: Always black, with no white markings
Use: Harness work
Features: Small in stature, it is compact yet strong and muscular; fine head, short legs with some feathering on the heels; hard feet of blue horn; tail and mane is thick and luxuriant and are rarely pulled or plaited.

The Friesian is one of Europe's oldest breeds, and, like the famous Friesian cattle, takes its name from its native Friesland, off the north coast of the Netherlands where a heavy horse is known to have existed as far back as 1,000 BC. The Roman historian Tacitus (AD 55-120) recorded the Friesian's existence and noted its value as an all-round, powerful utility horse. Descended from the primitive Forest Horse, and influential in many breeds, especially in British breeds such as the Fell (see page 64) and Dales (see page 56) ponies, and Shire horses (see page 90), during the Middle Ages, the Friesian carried Friesian and German knights to the Crusades. Today, magnificent black Friesians continue to maintain their qualities of strength, endurance and gentle nature that has been prized for over a thousand years. As a result of contact with eastern horses during the Crusades, and later through crosses with Andalucians (see page 130) and Barbs when the Netherlands became part of the Spanish dominions during the 16th and 17th centuries, the breed was further improved in stamina and movement.

Not surprisingly, the Friesian was in great demand to improve other breeds and to act as foundation stock. The German State Stud at Marbach used Friesians in the 17th century, while the Oldenberger (see page 201) was founded on Friesian stock. Despite its profound influences on British and European breeds, during the early part of the 20th century, the Friesian nearly became extinct. This was largely due to the popularity of trotting horses in the 19th

century: the Friesian had a trotting ability but the demand for lighter, faster horses meant that it became less suited to the agricultural work that it had hitherto performed. By 1913 only three Friesian stallions were left in their native Friesland: paradoxically, the breed was to be saved by the Second World War, when fuel shortages encouraged many Dutch farmers to return to horse power. A new breeding program was started using imported Oldenberger stallions, and the breed was revived. A new society was formed and in 1954 this was given a royal charter.

Today's Friesians are always black: incredibly versatile and willing, they are used for farming, are driven in harness, and are prized as dressage horses. In London a magnificent team of Friesians is still employed by the famous Knightsbridge department store Harrods where they make deliveries and promotional 'excursions' through the London streets. Furthermore, in England the fashion for traditional funerals requiring horse-drawn hearses, sees the Friesian very elegantly attired in black mourning feathers.

Furioso

Height: **15.2–16 hh (61-64 in.)**

Colors: Black, dark brown and dark bay are most common with white markings the exception rather than the rule

Use: Riding, harness, competition

Features: Thoroughbred-type head although the ears are more prominent; squared muzzle and large nostrils; good limbs with clean, large and well defined joints; upright pasterns betray carriage horse ancestry; hind legs are strong and hocks are low; quarters slope down from croup.

The Furioso, also known as the Furioso-North Star Breed, was first bred in Hungary in the 19th century and is one of the many breeds developed at the time when the Austro-Hungarian Empire was a dominant force – both politically and in equine terms – in Europe.

The studs at Mezohegyes, founded in 1785 by the Hapsburg Emperor Joseph II became the center for breeding first the Nonius (see page 197) and then later, the Furioso, which used Nonius mares as its

base. The breed derives its name from two English horses, a Thoroughbred (see page 122) called Furioso, who had been imported to Hungary by Count Karolyi in around 1840, and, North Star, who had Norfolk Roadster ancestry and who arrived in Hungary about three years later.

Furioso produced no fewer than 95 stallions at Mezohegyes, while North Star, who was himself the great-grandson of Waxy, the 1793 Derby winner, sired a great number of harness racers. At first, the Furioso and North Star lines were kept separate, but in 1885 they were inter-crossed, and from then on, the Furioso strain became predominant. Infusions of Thoroughbred blood continued to be introduced to upgrade the breed and the resulting Furioso was a horse of quality that could take part in all equestrian sports.

Hardy and intelligent, the Furioso is bred today across central and eastern Europe, from Austria, Hungary, the Czech Republic and Slovakia to Poland and Romania. Because they are bred across such a wide area, the different Furioso 'nationalities' can vary in size and color, and the heavier horses are often used for light draft and agricultural work. In Hungary, Furioso breeding is centered on the Apajpuszta Stud situated between the rivers Danube and Tisza. Strong and willing, the Furioso, like its relative the Nonius, is not built for speed, but it does excel at harness racing and at steeple chasing, where courage and strength are more prized than velocity.

Gelderlander

Height: 15.2–16.2 hh (61-65 in.)

Colors: Solid colors, usually chestnut, sometimes gray, often with white markings on legs and face

Use: Riding, harness, and light draft work

Features: Plain head on long, strong, slightly curved neck; good shoulders set on low, broad withers as appropriate for a harness horse; compact body; strong, long back; strong quarters short, strong legs; energetic action and proud carriage.

The Gelderlander is one of the most popular carriage horses in the Netherlands where it originated in the province of Gelder, and, along with the Groningen, is the chief influence on the make up of the Dutch Warmblood (see page 151).

The Gelderlander was first bred in the 19th century with the aim of producing a first class carriage horse that had both presence and action, and that was capable of light draft work and being ridden. Great emphasis was placed on producing a horse with a very equitable temperament, so local mares were crossed with stallions from Britain, including Cleveland Bays and Norfolk Roadsters; Nonius and Furiosos from Hungary; East Prussians from Poland; Orlov Trotters from Russia, and, Arabs from Egypt. Later, Oldenbergers and East Friesians were introduced into the breed and in 1900, Hackney blood was infused.

The modern Gelderlander is a very impressive carriage horse with an eye-catching, rhythmic, and lofty action and a tail carried high on strong quarters. While a few have become above-average show jumpers, it is in competition driving that these bright chestnut colored horses have really excelled.

Hack

The Hack – or Show Hack as it is known in Britain – is something of a British phenomenon, although it has been adopted by show ring exhibitors elsewhere in the world. It is also a breed that is easy to define on paper, but in practise, it is more difficult: what 'makes' a Hack is one of the most hotly debated ringside topics. But there is one point on which everyone agrees: they know a good Hack when they see one! The word Hack (like Hackney, see page 167) comes from the Norman-French word haquenée which was used to describe a horse for general riding purposes – as distinct from a war horse. In the 19th century, two types of Hack were recognized in Britain: the Covert Hack and the Park Hack. The Covert Hack was a good looking and elegant, even 'showy' Thoroughbred riding horse which carried its owner at a smooth 'hack canter' to the meet on hunting days, allowing him to be very fashionable and 'cut a dash'. His Hunter (see page 176) would have been ridden by his groom in advance and was ready waiting at the meet. Since the Hack was not required to carry the rider's weight for the full day's hunt, it was lighter in build than the Hunter: bone, strength and stamina were of less importance than

Height: Between 14.2 and 15.3 hh (57-61 in.) depending on class

Colors: Any solid color

Use: Riding, competition

Features: A neat head, without any concavity, tapering to the muzzle; long, elegant neck running smoothly into prominent withers; sloped shoulders; rounded quarters; long, graceful legs with 8 in. of bone expected below the knee; overall shape is that of a Thoroughbred.

elegance, presence, and smoothness of action. Covert Hacks no longer exist in either the hunting field (where motorized transport made them redundant) or in the show ring. The closest equivalent are to be seen in the show classes for riding horses.

The Park Hack was an even more elegant and refined horse on which riders superbly 'suited and booted' in the

height of fashion, paraded before admiring ladies – and critical gentlemen! In London's Hyde Park, Rotten Row was the place for showing off both one's clothes and the skill and beauty of the Hack: this horse needed to be very well mannered in order that the fashionable beau could strike just the right 'casual' pose by controlling his mount with one hand in a light, single-curb bit.

The modern Hack is expected to have all the attributes of the 19th century Hack: lightness, grace, and an example of perfect proportions. In action it must be straight and true, with the hind legs consistently 'tracking up' – falling into the imprints left by the forefeet. At the trot, the movement should be low and 'floating', with the toes extended without any 'dishing' or lifting of the knees. While elegance is of primary importance, 'blood weeds' (a weak insubstantial type of Thoroughbred which lacks bone and substance), overgrown riding ponies, and animals with a pronounced Arab character are not encouraged, because substance is every bit as desirable in the Hack as in the Hunter. In other words, a good front is essential.

The majority of entrants into Hack classes are Thoroughbreds (see page 122) – but some may be part-Arab or Anglo-Arabs

(see page 120). As well as classes for pairs, there are three classes for single Hacks: Small Hacks standing at 14.2–15 hh (47-60 in.); Large Hacks of 15–15.3 hh (160-63 in.), and, Ladies' Hacks between 14.2–15.3 hh (57-61 in.) which are shown under side-saddle. Hacks are shown at walk, trot, and canter – they are not required to gallop – and each rider must give an individual display of his Hack's ability in movements such as simple leg changes, a change of rein, a half pass to the left or right, a rein-back, and a halt with complete immobility. The training, production and presentation of the Show Hack is nothing less than an art, and in accordance with British conventions, the Hack is also 'test ridden' by the judge and is expected to give him or her an equally smooth and elegant ride.

Hackney Horse

The high-stepping Hackney horse – and the related Hackney pony – are perhaps the world's most impressive harness horses. Both horse and pony have their base in the tradition of English trotting horses of the 18th and 19th centuries (although the pony also has Fell influence) The name 'hackney' is derived from the Norman-French word *haquenée* which was used to describe a general-purpose riding horse, and had been in use in England for many centuries. The name was chosen as the breed appellation when a Society was formed at Norwich in 1883 in order to compile a stud book for English trotting horses.

Height: Hackney Horse: 14–15.3 hh (56-61 in.)
   Hackney Pony: up to 14 hh (56 in,)
Colors: Bay, brown, black and chestnut
Use: Driving
Features: Head is slightly convex in profile; small, neat ears; fine muzzle; large eyes; long neck rising almost vertically out of shoulders which are exceptionally strong; withers are quite low; compact body, but great depth to chest; feet are allowed to grow longer than usual to give 'snap' to action; fine, silky coat.

Trotting horses had been recognized as a variety for some years before this date, and were chiefly found in East Anglia, parts of Lincolnshire, and in East Yorkshire where they were known as Yorkshire trotters, Norfolk Roadsters, Norfolk Cobs, or even 'nag horses' – the old French word *haque* is related to the Spanish *haca* which means a 'nag' or gelding.

The best of the trotting horses – from both Norfolk and Yorkshire – traced their descent from Shales. Born in 1755, he was the son of the Thoroughbred Blaze (the great-grandson of the Darley Arabian, one of the three founding sires of the Thoroughbred and who was also related to Messenger, founder of the American Standardbred harness racer). From the middle of the 19th century, Hackney stallions were in great demand as improvers of native stock in many countries

and for producing military and carriage horses. By the end of the century, the popularity of horse shows led to a demand for stylish, high-stepping carriage horses, and in this role, with its lofty gait, the Hackney was supreme. With the advent of motor transport, demand for the Hackney went into decline.

Today, the original regional variations are gone, but the finest qualities of the trotting horses are combined in the modern Hackney which has both Arab and Thoroughbred blood. It is mostly seen in the show ring – where its extravagant and elevated trot is ideally suited.

While the Hackney horse shares the same common ancestry and indeed, the same stud book as its 'cousin', the Hackney pony, the latter is a real pony, not exceeding 14 hh (1.42 m), not just a small horse. The Hackney pony was essentially created by Christopher Wilson of Cumbria, who, in the 1880s, had created a distinct type based on trotting lines crossed with Fell Ponies (see page 64). The 'Wilson Ponies', as they were called, were restricted to their required height by being wintered on the fells where they were left to fend for themselves – a practice which also ensured a very hardy constitution.

Hanoverian

One of the most successful European warmbloods, the Hanoverian has a worldwide reputation as an excellent show jumper and dressage horse. The breed traces its origins back to the 17th century when Spanish, oriental and Neapolitan stallions were imported into Germany and crossed with local mares to create the Holsteiner (see page 174). The royal House of Hanover gave impetus to the 'local' breed: the white horse of Hanover appeared on the coat of arms of the Elector Ernst Augustus (1629-98) and the famous Royal Hanoverian Creams, with their distinctive pale, coffee-colored manes and tails, were bred at the Electress Sophia's royal residence at Herrenhausen. In 1714, George, Elector of Hanover became George I of England. He exported early 'Thoroughbreds' from England to upgrade the German stocks.

In 1735, George II founded the Stallion Depot at Celle where the aim was to create a core stock of strong stallions that when mated with local mares, would produce an all-purpose agricultural horse. The breeding program started by using 14 powerful coach horses, the black Holsteiners. The Thoroughbred was introduced to produce a lighter, better quality horse that could be

Height: 15.3– 16.2 (61-65 in.)
Colors: All solid colors
Use: Riding, competition
Features: Light, medium sized head; long neck running into big, sloping shoulders with pronounced withers; broad, powerful loins; muscular quarters with a flattening at the croup; powerful, symmetrical limbs with well-pronounced joints with good bone length below the knee on forelimbs.

used in harness or as a cavalry remount, as well as for agricultural work. From the outset, all the horses at Celle were registered, and branded with the distinctive stylized letter 'H', and by the end of the 18th century, detailed pedigrees were being kept.

During the Napoleonic Wars, the stock at Celle was depleted. When the stud reopened in 1816, there were only 30 stallions remaining from the 100 that had been kept there before the war. Numbers were rebuilt using more English Thoroughbred imports and horses from Mecklenburg (the stud to which the Celle horses had been evacuated for safety). Thoroughbred blood, which was regarded as an essential to safeguard stamina and courage, had always been strictly monitored and kept to a mere 2-3 % to avoid producing horses that were 'too-light'. By the mid 19th century, however, Thoroughbred influence had risen to around 35% and the Hanoverian was now too light for the agricultural work for which it was first intended.

New attempts were made to standardize the breeding of the heavier type by using indigenous lines within the Hanoverian breed. By the end of the First World War, Celle had 350 stallions, and by 1924, it had 500. But after the Second World War, the role of the horse in agriculture went into a decline and many breeders turned to producing competition riding horses. Some 'refugee' Trakehners (see page 234) from East Prussia found their way to Celle and were added to the stock, along with Thoroughbreds. These acted as a 'refining agent' on the Hanoverian: they lightened the still heavy-bodied horse and gave it a greater degree of movement – at the expense of some of its power. Today the Hanoverian shows no trace of the high knee movement that characterized the old Hanoverian carriage horse and they are renowned as show jumpers and dressage performers.

The breeding of Hanoverians is conducted under the auspices of the Society of Hanoverian Warmblood Breeders in Hanover, while the stallion depot at Celle, along with the affiliated stallion testing center at Westercelle, is maintained by the federal government of Niedesachsen.

Malapolski

Height: 15.3–16.2 hh (61–65 in.)
Colors: All solid colors
Use: Riding, larger version used for light draft work
Features: Strong, muscular body; wide, deep chest;
    tendency towards a concave face; eyes wide set;
    longish neck; prominent withers; long, straight
    back; slightly sloping croup; long, sloping
    shoulders and well-muscled legs; good joints; feet
    of tough horn.

The Malapolski, also known as the Polish Anglo-Arab, is a relatively recent breed which contains a good deal of oriental blood. It was developed from primitive local horses, with infusions of Furioso-Northstar, Thoroughbred, and Gidran Arabian blood.

There are two distinct 'versions' of the Malapolski: the differences are the result of the regions in which they are bred. The Sadecki has been greatly influenced by the Furioso, and while it makes a fine riding horse, it is often bigger and therefore used extensively in southwestern Poland on farms. The smaller Malapolski, the Darbowsko-Tarnowski, is also bred in the southwest of Poland but has received more influence from the Hungarian Gidran Arabian. All the Polish Warmbloods are also known as Wielkopolskis, but those horses, like the Malapolski, which are bred in certain areas of Poland, are still regarded as being of specific types.

The Malapolski is a quality riding horse with exceptional jumping abilities. Its calm and level character coupled with its great stamina make it a fine performer in sporting competitions.

Westphalian

Height: 16– 17.2 hh (64-69 in.)
Colors: All colors
Use: Riding, competition
Features: Noble head on a long neck; sloping shoulders and high withers; well muscled back and croup; strong legs with large joints.

Warmblood breeding in Germany is largely dominated by the Hanoverian Horse (see page 169): more than 7,000 mares are served annually by selected stallions and the type has become a guiding factor in warmblood breeding. Consequently, many other breeding regions in Germany use Hanoverian stallions to produce Hanoverian horses, but, there can be some differences in type. One such example is the Westphalian Horse.

Horses have been bred in Westphalia since Roman times and through the course of the centuries, wild horses survived in the marshy parts of the region that were not put to the plow. Until the 19th century, five herds of wild horses existed; the last marshy area in existence is the Merfelder-Bruch near Duelmen, which is home to the last herd of semi-wild horses in Germany.

The Westphalian was bred at the state stud in Warendorf in Westphalia, which was founded in 1826. In the early stages of its development, the Westphalian was based on Oldenburger (see page 201) blood with the addition of Anglo-Norman stallions, but these were not suited to working the Westphalian soil. Since the 1920s, the Westphalian breeding program has been based on Hanoverian blood with some Trakehner and Thoroughbred influence, with the aim of producing a large riding horse with a quiet temperament that could excel at shows and be used for pleasure riding.

The Westphalian is, in effect, a Hanoverian, but, they are also called Westfalisches Pferd. They can also sometimes be a little coarser in build: the

Westphalian is more of a 'coaching type', although it can also be used for riding. At the hacienda of La Escondida, in northeast Mexico, 15 Westphalians were imported by Guillermo Zambrano in 1978, and since then, the ranch has produced many outstanding show jumpers and dressage horses, including Romanow II.

The breeding of Westphalians is conducted under the auspices of the Westphalian Stud Book in Munster, while the federal government of Northrhine-Westphalia maintains the Warendorf stud of Westfalisches Pferd stallions, and where each year there is a spectacular parade.

173

Holsteiner

Height: **16–17 hh (64-68 in.)**
Colors: **All solid colors**
Use: **Riding, driving, competition**
Features: **Thoroughbred-type head, although of the plainer type; large, bright eyes; long, slightly arched neck; pronounced withers; powerful quarters and strongly muscled stifles, thighs and gaskins; short cannons; large, flat knees; forelegs set well apart with elbows clear of the body.**

The oldest of the German warmbloods, this breed takes its name from the Elmshorn district of Holstein, where the breeding of horses reaches back into the mists of time. By the 14th century, horse breeding in the region was largely the concern of the monasteries, in particular, the monastery at Uetersen which used the nearby marshes of Haseldorf on the River Elbe as its stud. The monastery was dedicated to producing war horses and 'tourney' (tournament) horses for which they received noble patronage from the kings of Denmark and the dukes of Schleswig-Holstein. Later, the local horses received an infusion of Spanish, Eastern, and Neapolitan blood which made them lighter in build, and from the 16th to the 18th century, the Holsteiner was in great demand across Europe as a tough carriage or coach horse.

Holsteiners were also being used to improve other German warmblood breeds such as the Hanoverian (see page 169) and the Westphalian (see page 173). In 1680 at the

Holstein royal stud at Esserom, the Holsteiner stallion Mignon was used to begin breeding the famous cream horses that became the pride of the electors of Hanover. When the English crown passed to the House of Hanover in 1714, these cream horses formed part of the stable of the Royal Mews in London until the 1920s.

In the 19th century, two imported bloodlines were introduced: the English Thoroughbred (see page 122) and Yorkshire Coach Horses. The Thoroughbred would make the Holsteiner more compact and shorter legged, and the prevailing 'Roman nose' was straightened out, while the galloping ability was also improved. The Yorkshire Coach Horse brought the characteristic high and wide gait and the even temperament to the Holsteiner, so it now had a reputation as a fine dual-purpose carriage and riding horse. The breed continued to be developed along these lines at the Traventhal Stud founded by the Prussians in 1867, but, when this closed down, the Society of Breeders of Holstein Horses in Elmshorn assumed

responsibility for the breed, which, like all European warmbloods, is subject to rigorous performance testing.

Since World War II additional Thoroughbred blood has been introduced to produce a lighter, multipurpose riding and competition horse, who can gallop and jump extremely well: Meteor and Tora are just two examples of the fine German show jumpers which have achieved international fame. Powerfully built, the Holsteiner is a good-tempered, intelligent, willing, and very handsome horse.

Hunter

Height: Variable, from 15–18 hh (60-72 in.) but on average, 16–16.2 hh (64-66 in.)

Colors: All colors

Use: Riding, hunting, show ring

Features: All the qualities of a riding horse with substance, strength and good bone: well slopped shoulders, compact body, deep girth, powerful quarters, cannon bones aligned with hocks, clean joints. No set pattern for head but should be of quality and have an alert, intelligent expression.

A Hunter is any horse used for the purpose of riding to hounds. It is a type of horse and, depending on the country in which it is used and the terrain which it has to cross, Hunters may vary. Consequently, Hunters do not have 'shared' characteristics – for example, color – and so the Hunter is not a breed. Nevertheless, a good Hunter is one that is sound, well-proportioned and with all the conformational attributes of a top-class riding horse. These qualities are further combined with courage, agility, jumping ability, stamina, and a robust constitution.

The finest Hunter horses are bred in countries which themselves have a long tradition of the sport, such as the U.K. and Ireland. Increasingly though, Hunters bred in countries such as the United States where Thoroughbred influence is important, are producing Hunters of great quality. In general, the greater the amount of Thoroughbred blood, the greater the speed and scope of the horse: In the largely open pasturelands of the English shires (the Midlands which include Warwickshire, Leicestershire, Northamptonshire, and parts of Lincolnshire) Thoroughbred horses capable of jumping fences are favored, while in more enclosed country, such as plowed fields or on hills, a powerful, shorter-legged, half- or three-quarter bred horse is considered more suited to the terrain.

Thoroughbred crosses with Cleveland Bays (see page 144) – a hunter in its own right – results in fast horses that can still carry a very substantial rider (up to 252 lb) for a full days hunting across heavy clay soils and over large obstacles. Other heavyweight Hunters are the result of Thoroughbred and English heavy horse crosses, such as the Clydesdale (see page 99), but equally good horses are also produced from crosses and second crosses with British native pony breeds. Some of the larger British ponies themselves, such as the Welsh Cob (see page 89) are also at home in the hunt where they can easily carry a lighter adult in most hunting countries. Irish Hunters, considered by many as the finest cross-country horses in the world are based on a Thoroughbred/Irish Draft (see page 179) cross. These horses are hunted as three- and four-year-olds, and almost always in a plain, snaffle bridle.

A profound influence on the breeding of Hunters, encouraging the breeding of a particular type, are the Hunter showing classes which are among the most prestigious of all in the show ring. Ridden Hunter classes are divided into eight

categories: in each category the horses are galloped, shown stripped (without tack), and in Britain and Ireland – though not in the U.S.A. and Canada – are ridden by the judge. Weight classes are divided into light, middle, and, heavy weight. This does not refer to the size of the horse, but to the weight it is capable of carrying, which is linked to the amount of bone it possesses. This is measured around the cannon bone. There are also classes for small Hunters of 15.2 hh (61 in.) or under; Ladies' Hunters, which are ridden side-saddle; novice, for horses that have not yet won a certain level of prize money; four-year-old classes, and, classes for working Hunters, which are expected to jump a course of between eight and 12 natural fences. Conformation and manners are all assessed by the Hunter judge, who is also looking for quality and substance in the right proportions. But a champion Hunter must not only be as perfect as possible when standing still: movement and ride are also assessed by the Hunter judge.

Irish Draft

Height: **15–17 hh (60-68 in.)**
Colors: **All solid colors**
Use: **Hunting, light draft work**
Features: **Small head in relation to size of body; deep-chested, though body may be a little long; distinctive oval ribcage – horses should not be 'slab-sided'; long, arching neck and sloping shoulders; withers set well back; quarters slope downwards from the croup to meet the tail which is carried high in movement; strong, powerfully muscled hind thighs and large hock joints; minimal feathers.**

Without doubt one of the finest cross-country horses in the world (and the foundation of the great Irish Hunter) the Irish Draft's development started in the 12th century when native Irish horses were upgraded by heavy French and Flemish horses which were imported to the country following the Anglo-Norman invasion of 1172. The strong mares that resulted were further improved by introducing Andalucian (see page 130) blood which produced draft horses that were used for every kind of work on small Irish farms, but were also versatile enough to be used under saddle. Once common all over rural Ireland, the breed declined during the famines of 1847.

Attempts were made to improve the remaining stock through crosses with Clydesdale (see page 99) and Shires (see page 90), but these added a coarseness to the Irish and also were responsible for the breed becoming somewhat 'tied-in' below the knee, a fault that has taken some time to eradicate. By this time the 'old' Irish Draft was a low built animal standing no more than 15.2-15.3 (61-62 in.), with upright shoulders, dropping quarters and a goose-rump. Nonetheless, these horses could trot in harness and canter and gallop under saddle, and they were said to be fine jumpers who were fearless of even the greatest obstacles.

The introduction of Thoroughbred (see

page 122) blood in the 19th century gave the Irish Draft quality and speed, without removing any of its innate hunting abilities. The breed was also substantially improved when stallion subsidies were made in 1904 and breeding encouraged. In 1917 a *Book for Horses of Irish Draft Type* was opened with 375 mares and 44 stallions entered.

However, the breed declined with the advent of mechanization in farming, and numbers suffered further during World War I when many of the finest mares were requisitioned by the army for military use as 'Gunners'. Clean-legged, they did not develop the 'grassy heels' suffered by many horses in the wet of the Flanders mud and because of their ability to thrive on meager army rations, many Irish Drafts which left their homeland as gun teams in 1914 entered Brussels in the

Ceremonial Parade in 1918. In the 1960s, exports to Europe for slaughter led to near extinction in its homeland until legislation was introduced in 1964 to curb the trade.

Fortunately, Ireland regards their horses as part of their national treasures and in 1976 the Irish Draft Society was formed and which operates a grading system to ensure quality animals are produced for registration. When crossed with Thoroughbred mares, the Irish Draft passes on to its progeny its bone, substance, size, and athleticism. Today, the Irish Draft is a bigger horse than a century ago, with most standing 16 hh (64 in.) – while stallions easily reach 17 hh (68 inches).

Kabardin

The Kabardin is a little mountain horse from the Caucasus which has been regarded as a breed since the 16th century. In the 17th century, these horses became more widely famous and were considered the finest mountain horse in the whole of central Asia. Bred by mountain tribesmen, using indigenous mountain breeds with infusions of Turkmene and Karabakh blood (both of which are 'southern' Russian breeds), along with Arab genes in the 19th century, the Karbadin is the product of centuries of selective breeding for survival under the harshest conditions. Later the Kabardin was crossed with neighboring Karabakh horses, and with Thoroughbred (see page 122) mares to produce the bigger – and faster – Anglo-Kabardins.

Today, the finest Kabardin horses are bred at the Malokarachayev and the Malkin Studs where in spring, breeders form *kosyaks*, small herds of around 20 mares in the charge of a sire who protects them from wolves and other sires. Early in May the herds begin to move uphill, and as the snow line recedes they climb higher and higher until they reach their summer pastures where the only supplement to their diet is salt. Early in August, the stallions are separated from their herds and all the

Height: 15–15.2 hh (50-61 in.)
Colors: Dark bay, bay, and black predominate
Use: Riding, trekking, harness, and light draft work
Features: Considered to be a 'perfect mountain horse' its features include those often considered defects in other mounts: straight shoulders, flat withers, narrow poll, ear turn slightly inwards, hind legs are sickle-shaped, but forelegs are a good feature being clearly defined with short cannons. Unbelievably hard hooves make shoeing a problem, but most Kabardins go unshod on even the hardest ground. Luxurious mane and tail.

mares are brought together; in September, with the first snows, the herds begin their migration downhill to spend the winters outdoors in enclosures where they receive additional hay. Weaning takes place in November and yearlings are divided according to sex, and grazed and trained separately.

The Kabardin has developed characteristics that are suited to its terrain and to the rigors of the climate – characteristics which in other mounts would be considered defects. The blood of the Kabardin has a heightened oxidizing capacity which makes them supreme performers at very high altitudes: they can climb – with a rider – to heights of more than 16, 500 ft, and unlike other breeds, do not need to recover from their exertions. Their hearts, lungs, tendons, ligaments, and muscles are immensely strong and efficient!

To compensate for their often meager diets, when there is food, Kabardins quickly accumulate body fat to keep them going. Their bodies are dense, massive, and elongated, their backs are well-muscled, short and straight, and the quarters slope away from the rounded croup. The loins,

while very strong, are often slightly concave. By Western standards the withers are flat and the shoulders are straight – which accounts for their high action. Some Kabardin pace naturally: it is said that this gait was passed on to all horses of Mongol blood by the favorite mount of the mighty Genghiz Khan. The head profile is 'Roman-nosed' and between the ears the poll is particularly narrow and the occiput ill-defined. The hind legs are often sickle-shaped – which in a mountain horse is a great advantage. The hooves are also unbelievably hard: most Kabardin are left unshod, even in the hardest of mountain terrains.

Kabardins have the most remarkable abilities and thrive in the most difficult terrains, often at extremely high altitudes. They will happily cross steep mountain passes, travel through deep snows and icy rivers, for they are seemingly impervious to cold. They rarely stumble, even when trotting or cantering downhill, are undeterred by falling rocks, and they have an unerring sense of direction: the mountain tribesman know their mounts will find their herds within a mile – even through the darkness of night or heavy mountain mists. While they are not particularly impressive on the race course, over distances they are rarely beaten. In 1946 a major test of the performance of Russian breeds was organized in Moscow: a 155-mile ride – with the final mile to be covered at a trot – was won by the Kabardin stallion Ali-Kadym in just 25 hours.

Knabstrup

Height: 15.2– 15.3 hh (60-61 in.)

Colors: Spotted

Use: Riding

Features: Conformation varies and is closer in character to that of the Appaloosa (the line of the back from the wither is peculiar to Knabstrup and some Appaloosa strains);the neck is strong and well-muscled, but tending to shortness; sparse mane and tail; spotting extends down legs to feet; cannons are short, knees are flat and wide; horn of feet often has vertical stripes.

The Knabstrup traces back to a spotted Spanish mare called Flaebehoppen which translates as 'Flaebe's horse'. She was bought by a butcher in 1808 (who was called Flaebe) from a Spanish officer during the Napoleonic Wars and who was then sold on to the founder of the breed, Judge Lunn. Flaebehoppen was renowned for her speed and endurance, and at his estate in Knabstrup, Denmark, Judge Lunn bred her with Frederiksborg stallions and produced a line of spotted horses that were not as substantial as the Frederiksborg, but were very much in demand for their color and ability. These were the 'Old Knabstrups': they had more of a harness conformation which was evident in the shoulders and short neck. They were also stronger and more raw-boned than the modern horse, but they were equally tough and quick to learn.

These qualities, coupled with their color (which was originally white with brown or black spots of varying size covering the whole body) made them popular as circus horses. Injudicious breeding for color rather than conformation led to the deterioration of the breed and it nearly died out. The 'Old Knabstrup' is now rare but over the past 50 years, improvements to the breed have been made, and the modern

Knabstrup is a much more substantial, better quality horse than the 'Old Knabstrup' of the 19th century: the best examples of the breed have well-rounded quarters with good muscular development. To a large extent, the conformation defects that occurred in the limbs have also been corrected and today they also occur in a greater range of colors. The sparse mane and tail appears to be a characteristic accompaniment of spotted coats: they are found in both the 'Old' and modern Knabstrup as well as in the Appaloosa (see page 134).

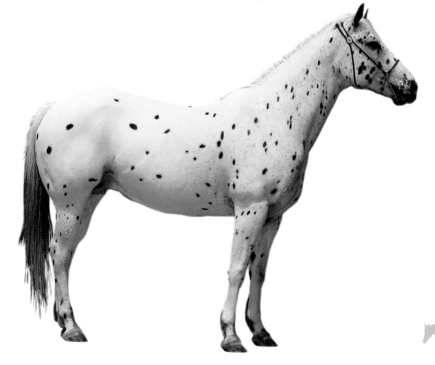

Lipizzaner

Height: 15–16 hh (60-64 in.)

Colors: White, but solid colors including black, bay and chestnut can also be found

Use: Haute école dressage; harness

Features: Arab influence in head is often apparent, but the 'ram-like' profile of the Spanish horse can also be seen; body is compact and deep with considerable depth through the girth; short neck; withers are not pronounced and shoulders are well suited to both riding and harness; action tends to be high rather than low and long; powerful quarters; short, powerful limbs with flat joints; hard feet; silky mane and tail.

The Lipizzanner is to the equine world what Rudolph Nureyev was to ballet: even those who have never been on a horse could probably name this, one of the world's most beautiful horses. Indeed, the Lipizzaners at the famous Spanish Riding School in Vienna perform the most beautiful of 'dances' including the famous leaps called 'airs above the ground'.

This ancient breed takes its name from the Lipizza (Lipica) Stud, in Slovenia, where it originated and is still bred. Once part of the great Austro-Hungarian Empire, the Lipizza Stud was founded in 1580 by the Archduke Charles II. The formation stock of the breed were nine Spanish stallions and 24 mares which were imported from the Iberian Peninsula with the aim of providing suitably grand horses for the ducal stables in Graz and the court stables in Vienna. Other studs were also founded, the most important of which were at Piber, near Graz in Austria and Kladruby in the Czech Republic. Founded in 1572 this stud is the oldest in Europe, and is the home of the Kladruber carriage horse. Also based on Spanish stock, the Kladruber was to influence the Lipizzaner quite considerably. The Spanish Riding School in Vienna – so called because it had used Spanish horses from the outset – had been established eight years earlier in a wooden arena located next to the Imperial Palace. Today the school is housed in the Winter Riding Hall, built on the orders of Charles VI and completed in 1735. The horses that can be seen there today can trace back to six principal foundation stallions: Pluto (born 1765) was a white horse of Spanish descent obtained form the Royal Danish Court Stud; Conversano (born 1767) was a black Neapolitan, while Neapolitano (born 1790) was a bay Neapolitan from Polesina, both of which were said to have been bred from Spanish horses. Maestoso (born 1819) was a white Kladruber horse bred at the famous

Hungarian stud at Mezohegyes; Favory, a dun born at the Kaldruby Stud in 1779; and Siglavy, who is believed to have been an Arab born in 1810. The foundation mares in most cases were of Spanish origin.

Over the years, stallions were frequently exchanged between the studs at Lipizza, Piber and Kladruby, but when the Spanish Riding School opened 'for the education of the nobility in the art of horsemanship' horses from the Lipizza stud were found to be more amenable to training in the haute école and they began to be regarded as a separate breed. Although the Lipizza Stud's policy was always to breed white horses until the 18th century – considered to be the most suitably dignified color for the Imperial house – other colors including black, bays, and duns, as well as magnificently spotted, piebald and skewbald did exist.

The modern Lipizzaners, which appear at the Riding School in Vienna, have since 1920 been bred at Piber. Fewer than ten are selected each year and their training takes between four and six years. They are white, although the foals are born black or brown. There are also occasional bays, and while these are not kept for breeding, by tradition, one bay is kept at the Riding School. The 'Piber Lipizzaner' generally stands a little over 15 hh (60 in.) and is a compact, very strongly limbed horse, powerful in the quarters and neck and often featuring the 'ram-like' profile of its Spanish ancestors.

As well as the Spanish Riding School's Piber Lipizzaners, Lipizzaners are bred throughout Hungary, Romania, Slovakia and the Czech Republic. While all of the studs maintain the six stallion lines on which the breed was founded, variations in type do occur and the Piber type is by no means predominant. All Lipizzaners are used under saddle, but outside the 'hot-house' Piber stud, they are also used for harness work and some can still be seen working on farms.

Mangalarga

In 1541, Alvar Nuñez landed near Santa Caterina on the Brazilian coast with a fleet carrying a number of horses – Alter-Reals from Portugal. Some –or all –of these horses either escaped or were set free, spreading out and breeding in the same way as the descendants of the Spanish horses that landed in and near the Argentine. The modern descendants of these Portuguese horses are similar to their cousins the Criollo (see page 148), but are smaller, and throughout the different parts of Brazil, different types appear. The Brazilian *Crioulo* can be found in northeast

Height: 14–16 hh (56-60 in.)
Colors: Chestnut, bay, roan, and gray
Use: Riding, stock work, endurance riding
Features: Long head; short, strong back; powerful quarters; low set tail; long legs.

Brazil where it is known as the *Nordestino* and in Goias State, as the *Courraleiro*. These two varieties are very hardy horses and able to survive on minimal rations. A further – and better – variety of the Crioulo is bred in the Rio Grande do Sul region, from which it takes its name.

The Mangalarga is a 'cousin' of the Crioulo: in the 19th century, Brazil imported selected stallions from Spain and Portugal which were used to upgrade the native stocks. One of the best stallions, called Sublime, was sent to stud in the Minas Gerais, where he founded the Mangalarga breed which is known locally as the Junquiera. The Mangalarga is a larger horse than the Crioulo and has longer legs. It is also distinguished by its peculiar gait, the *marcha* which is described as being halfway between a trot and a canter.

Attempts have been made to improve the Mangalargas with warmblood stallions, and the most successful crossbreeds for riding purposes have come from Arab (see page 113) Anglo-Arab (see page 120), Thoroughbred (see page 122) and Trakehner (see page 234) stallions.

In 1840, Cassiano Campolino also set out to improve the Mangalarga by selective breeding: this was so successful that a new variety, the slightly heavier Campolino came into existence and now flourishes in and around the state of Rio de Janeiro where they make excellent riding horses and are known for their great endurance which far exceeds that of imported horses.

Missouri Fox Trotter

The Missouri Fox Trotter is one of America's oldest and least known breeds. It is one of the trio of American gaited horses – the other two being the American Saddlebred (see page 126) and the Tennessee Walking Horse (see page 231). The breed was established in around 1820 when settlers moving westwards across the Mississippi River from the hills and plantations of Tennessee, Kentucky and Virginia made their homes in the Ozark Mountains of Missouri and Arkansas.

The most famous of the breeding families were the Alsups who bred the Brimmer line of horses descended from racehorses of the same name; the Kissees, who established the Diamond and Fox strains, and the Dunns, who produced Old Skip.

These families took with them their Thoroughbred horses (see page 122), Arabs (see page 113) and Morgans (see page 195) and the mares were then bred to the fastest sires. Originally, the horses were bred to race, but Puritan religious zeal put an end to such a frivolous pastime. The Ozark breeders instead turned their efforts to producing a fixed type of utility horse that would comfortably carry a rider at a steady speed over rough terrain. Following infusions of Saddlebred and Tennessee

Height: **14–16 hh (56–64 in.)**
Colors: All solid colors, but chestnut predominates.
Use: Riding
Features: A strong, compact horse with an attractive, tapered head with flared nostrils; arched neck; short strong back; deep in girth; muscular quarters; good length from hip to hock; hind legs are quite heavily built but well spaced: shanks are longer than normal; good feet are a feature of the breed.

Walking Horse blood, the result was a very sure-footed, smooth-moving horse with a unique gait, the fox trot.

The fox trot gait is a 'broken gait performed': this means that it performs an active walk in front, while trotting behind, and the hind feet step down and slide over the track of the forefeet. The sliding action – which should be perfectly straight – reduces concussion in the lower limbs and reduces the amount of movement in the back which means it stays very level. The only things that 'bobs' up and down rhythmically are the head and the tail. The result is that the rider sits comfortably in the saddle without feeling any of the action. The Missouri Fox Trotter can maintain this gait for long distances at around 5-8 mph and for short distances at a speedy 10 mph. Other gaits performed are a walk in strict four-time beat where the hind feet distinctly over-stride the front track, and the canter.

The Breed Society is very strict in overseeing the breed and its training: artificial training aids or 'appliances' such as false tails or tail sets (which give a high upright carriage to the tail) are not permitted to accentuate the natural gait. Excessive weighting of the feet with specially designed shoes is also forbidden, and any marks or sores around the coronets which indicate the use of chains mean that horses and riders are immediately disqualified. In show classes, where the Missouri Fox Trotter is ridden in western gear, 40% of marks are awarded for the fox trot and 20% each for the walk, canter and for general conformation. Outside the show ring, the Missouri Fox Trotter is equally sure-footed which makes it an ideal and very popular trail riding horse.

Morab

The Arab has long been acknowledged as a preeminent upgrading influence in the breed structure of the world's horses. When crossed with the Thoroughbred (see page 122) it created the Anglo-Arab. The equivalent horse in America, which uses the Morgan (see page 195) in place of the Thoroughbred, is the Morab.

Although history's first Morab was Golddust, born in 1855 and registered in the Morgan Registry as No. 70, the name Morab is said to have been coined by the American newspaper magnate, William Randolph Hearst. In the 1920s, Hearst used two Arab (see page 113) stallions on his Morgan mares to produce horses to work on his San Simeon Ranch in California.

The most hotly debated Morab issue is their status as a breed: some say they are part-bred, other term them half-breeds. But to others, Morabs which are the progeny or Morgan-Arabian breeding, are neither half-Morgans or half-Arabs but a very distinct breed. The Morab Horse Association (MHA) in the United States has claimed full breed status for the horses of Arab-Morgan cross: it seeks the acceptance of 25%Morgan-75% Arab breed standard for registrable Morabs.

Height: 14.3–15.3 hh (57-61 in.)

Colors: Solid colors

Use: Riding, ranch work

Features: Full, silky mane; 'Arab' shoulders; broad chest; withers are not defined; strong back; straight croup; tail set high; wide across hips; good feet but in most cases, hocks are a little too far off the ground; forearms long and muscular.

The MHA and the International Morab Registry (IMR) maintain detailed registries and archives. There is an also a breed standard, and although this really consists of generalizations that are applicable to all 'well-bred' horses, it does state that the shape of the hindquarters and the angle of the pelvis in the Morab are significantly different to other breeds.

Today's Morabs, with a century of breeding behind them, combine the strength of the Morgan with the refinement of the Arab. They have a shorter back than most other breeds, but this is combined with the longer croup of the Morgan which gives the Morab great strength and a smooth gait which combine to allow it to excel at competitive and endurance events.

Owners, breeders and fans of the Morab all cite its intelligence and its dependable nature which makes them ideal mounts for children and novice riders, as well as more spirited competitive riders.

Morgan

The Morgan is one of America's first documented breeds and whose history, like that of the Quarter horse (see page 213) is part of the history of the country itself. Unlike the Quarter horse though, the Morgan owes its existence to a single, phenomenal stallion, Justin Morgan. This, the undisputed sire of the first American breed was a dark bay horse born sometime between 1789 and 1793, in West Springfield, Massachusetts and stood no more than 14 hh (56 inches). He was also originally called Figure, until he came into the possession of Justin Morgan in 1795, a schoolmaster (although some say he was

Height: 14.2–15.2 hh (57-61 in.)

Colors: Bay, brown, black and chestnut

Use: Riding, driving, draught, competition

Features: Medium-sized, head with straight profile or just slightly dished – never Roman –nosed; large nostrils; well crested neck; clearly defined withers which are slightly higher than the point of the hip; strong, sloped shoulders; short, broad and well muscled back; large, rounded barrel; deep and wide chest; 'perfect' quarters; short cannon bones; short pasterns that are not too sloping; round feet of smooth, dense horn; long flowing tail that reaches the ground when horse is still.

195

an innkeeper) who took the horse in lieu of debts owed to him and took him home to Randolph Center, Vermont, where he was put to work in the plow. Poor old Justin Morgan, it seems, was passed from owner to owner several times – and with each one he endured plenty of hard work – until he ended up with a farmer Levi Bean, who assigned the horse the duty of pulling a muck spreader.

Little is known of Justin Morgan's background: some claim he was a Welsh Cob (see page 84), while another account says he was sired by a celebrated, pre-Revolutionary racer called True Briton. The only true certainty is that Justin Morgan possessed an incredibly robust constitution, extraordinary strength, and great speed. For not only did he work all day on farms in the biting cold winters of the north-eastern states, he was a regular at weight-hauling matches and races. In saddle or in harness, it is claimed that Justin Morgan was never beaten. His reputation spread across the region and he was in great demand as a stud. Soon his descendants, who apparently inherited his qualities – including his diminutive size and dark coloring – were spread across New England. His most famous sons were Sherman, Woodbury, and Bullrush, and all modern Morgans trace their ancestry to Justin Morgan through them.

The modern Morgan is no doubt a much more refined horse than Justin Morgan but it is still as spirited and courageous, intelligent, hard-working and versatile, powerful and as possessed of great stamina as their founding sire. The Morgan's compact size and happy nature has also helped to make it one of the most popular breeds in the U.S.A.

Nonius

Height: 15.3–16.2 hh (61-65 in.)

Colors: Bay and brown predominate but blacks and chestnut shades occur

Use: Riding, carriage

Features: Head is that of an honest, half-bred horse; neck is well formed, though not long or elegant; sloped shoulders and well defined withers; strong back and quarters, sometimes inclined to slope away from the croup; short legs but very strong.

The founder of the breed, Nonius Senior, was foaled at Calvados in northern France in 1810, said to be from an English half-bred stallion out of a Norman mare. During the Napoleonic Wars, Nonius was captured by the Hungarian cavalry following Napoleon's defeat at Leipzig in 1813 and taken to the Mezohhegyes Stud, where he produced 15 outstanding stallions out of a variety of mares.

Nonius was not, apparently, the most attractive of horses: he stood at just over 16.1 hh (64 in.), had a coarse, heavy head, with small eyes and 'mule' ears. He also had a short neck, long back, narrow pelvis and a low set tail. Nevertheless, he proved to be a prolific sire, consistently producing offspring that were far superior to himself in both conformation and action.

In the 1860s Thoroughbred blood was introduced and the breed was divided into two types: large carriage or light farm horses, and the smaller Nonius type which carries a little more Arab blood, for riding and light harness work. By this time the breed had also established its tendency to mature late – at six years old – but also to be commensurately long-lived.

National Show Horse

Height: 14.3–17 hh (57–86 in.)
Colors: Black, bay, chestnut, gray and pinto
Use: Riding, showing
Features: Long neck without pronounced crest, set high on shoulders; small head with straight or slightly concave profile; pronounced withers; short back with relatively level top line; short cannon bones in front legs; long, well-angled pasterns in rear legs; high-set tail.

The National Show Horse is a relatively new breed appellation: the result of crosses between Arabs (see page 113) and American Saddlebreds (see page 126), these horses have been around for some time. But it was not until the 1980s when a group of American enthusiasts formed an organization dedicated to the breed, that the National Show Horse was formally established. Until 1982, the association allowed open registration to form a pool of horses that would become the foundation of the new breed. Today, there are specific rules regarding registration. Three types of stallions and three types of mares are permitted: these must be American Saddlebreds, Arabs or National Show Horses, and they must also be registered with their appropriate registry. While any combination of the three breeds can be used to produce a National Show Horse, any resulting foals must meet blood content requirements ranging from 25-99% Arabian.

The qualities that are required in a National Show Horse include balance and power in the hindquarters and elevated front with the forelegs showing both flexion and extension. The relatively small head must have a straight profile or be slightly concave, but a 'Roman-nose' profile is discouraged. Thanks to its American Saddlebred ancestry, the National Show Horse is also one of the newest gaited horse breeds and is shown in three- and five-gaited classes. Like the Saddlebred, it can do the stepping pace: this takes its name from the fact that the horse's hind foot steps down just before the front foot of the same stride strikes the ground. The horse always has either one or two feet on the ground and suspension occurs first with the hind legs as they change places, then with the front legs and produces a very 'dainty' showy appearance. In some instances, the National Show Horse also performs the rack or 'singlefoot' – where only one foot is on the ground at any time and there is a moment of complete suspension when all four feet are off the ground.

In addition to gaited classes in the show rings, the National Show Horse is shown in Hunter, and Hunter Pleasure, English Pleasure, Pleasure Driving, Country Pleasure, Fine Harness, Western Pleasure, Show Hack and Equitation classes. Its all-round abilities and good looks are set to make this, one of the newest American breeds, a firm favorite across the world.

Hessian

Height: 16–17 hh (64–68 in.)
Colors: All solid colors
Use: Riding, competition
Feaures: Strong horse, ideally suited to riding and sport

The Hessian is one of the less well-known German warmblood breeds. Hesse has been a center for horse breeding for centuries, but the state stud at Dillenberg was not established until 1869, so consequently, local farmers concentrated on breeding light draught horses for which there was a great demand until the advent of mechanization removed the need for horses in agricultural work.

The transition from the warmblooded horse with predominantly Oldenburger (page 201) bloodlines, and with its characteristic 'Dillenberg Ram nose' – a distinct convex head profile – into the modern sports horse began in the mid-20th century. Using Hanoverians (page 169), Westphalians (page 173), Trakehners (page 234), as well as English Thoroughbreds (page 122) and Anglo-Arabs (page 120) to add refinement, the modern Hessian emerged. A very elegant horse, its temperament makes it ideally suited to both sport riding and pleasure riding. Breeding continues to take place at the Dillenberg Stud in tandem with private Hessian stallion owners who are organized into the Vereiningen Hessischer Hengsthalte.

Oldenburger

The Oldenburger is the heaviest of the German warmbloods and can be traced back to the 17th century. Based on the Friesian (see page 160), and developed on the vast grasslands of Oldenburg, Germany, the breed was established largely through the efforts of Count Anton Gunther von Oldenburg (1603-67). Oldenburgers today still carry the brand mark of a letter 'O' with a ducal coronet, on their near-side quarters.

The Count imported Spanish and Neapolitan horses – which both had backgrounds of Barb blood – along with his own gray stallion, Kranic, to develop a breed of good, strong and versatile carriage horses that could also be used for farm work. In the last part of the 18th century, half-bred English stallions were also introduced to refine the breed, and then, in the 19th century, breeders introduced Thoroughbreds (see page 122), Cleveland Bays (see page 144), Hanoverians (see page 169), and French-Norman blood. The result was a *karossierpferd*, a heavily built coach horse standing 17 hh. In spite of its massive

Height: 16.2–17.2 hh (65-69 in.)

Colors: All solid colors but chestnuts and grays are unusual.

Use: Riding, driving

Features: Neck is long and very strong, reflecting coach horse ancestry; long shoulders; head is plain, with straight profile although there is a tendency to a 'Roman nose'; short-legged with plenty of bone; a strong back; good depth of girth; quarters and hind limbs exceptionally strong; tail is set and carried high; stallions are tested before licensing and particular attention is paid to the feet which must be well open at the heels, sound and in large enough proportions to the horse.

size and build, the Oldenburger was an early-maturing animal, a very unusual feature in such a large horse.

As the demand for heavy coach horses declined with the introduction of motor vehicles, the breed began to be developed for agricultural work. When demand for this type of horse collapsed after World War II, the emphasis shifted to producing a riding horse. A Norman stallion called Condor who carried 70% Thoroughbred blood was used, along with a Thoroughbred called Lupus. Since then out-crosses have been mainly Thoroughbred but with some Hanoverian, in order to maintain the even temperament for which the breed is famous.

While still a big, powerful animal, the Oldenburger is not built for speed, but is well suited to dressage on account of its regular paces. The action is straight and rhythmical, although because of its coaching ancestry, is inclined to be a little high. But this does not disadvantage the dressage horse, or indeed the show jumper,

at which the Oldenburger can also excel. Strong stocky legs are needed to carry such a large-bodied horse: the joints are big, the cannons fairly short and the bone measurement is around 9 inches. Under Acts of 1819, which were amended in 1897 and 1923, the responsibility for the Oldenburger breed and the licensing of stallions lies with the Society of Breeders of the Oldenburg Horse. The society pursues a rigorous policy of careful selection and testing to ensure a uniformity of type in the breed.

Orlov Trotter

The oldest and most popular breed in Russia, the Orlov Trotter dates back to 1778 when Count Alexei Orlov (1737-1808) began a breeding program at the Khrenov Stud. The white Arab stallion, Smetanka, was used along with Dutch, Mecklenburg and Danish mares. Among the five progeny was Polkan I who was the sire of the Orlov breed's foundation stallion, a gray stallion called Bars I who was born in 1784. Bars I was described by contemporaries as a tall horse of elegant conformation with outstanding action, especially in the trot. He was mated with

Height: 16 hh (64 in.)

Colors: Gray predominates, black and bay are also common, chestnut rare.

Use: Trotting, driving, riding

Features: A tall, lightly built horse with strong shoulders; long 'swan neck' set high on shoulders; long back but plenty of depth in girth; low withers; strong legs with good bones and slight feathering; slightly heavy head.

Arab, Danish, and Dutch mares, as well as English half-breds and Arab-Mecklenburg crosses. Thereafter, the policy was to inbreed Bars I and his sons to establish the desired type.

By the beginning of the 19th century the Orlov Trotters were widely known: an important part of their improvement came with the systematic tests of the breed on race courses. Trotting races in Moscow had been held since 1799: these took place usually in winter with horses racing with light sleighs. From 1834, as a result of crossing Orlovs with American Standardbreds, a faster Orlov emerged.

Although they were used on the race course, Orlov Trotters were never purely for racing: they have also been used for drawing coaches, phaetons, and of course, the famous Russian troikas. The troika is the Russian method of harnessing three horses side by side. The center horse works at a fast trot while the out-spanners are bent outward by tight side reins, and they must gallop or canter to keep up with the center horse. For this reason, Orlov Trotters for breeding have always been chosen not only for speed, but for their other qualities: a good height, with a light but substantial frame, and an attractive conformation coupled with a sound constitution.

There are five basic types of modern Orlov Trotter, with the type varying according to the stud at which the animals are bred. The best and most characteristic Orlovs are those which are bred at Khrenov, and these are regarded as the 'classical Orlov'. Others are bred at Perm in the Urals, Novotomnikov, and at Tula and Dubrov. The Orlovs bred here are closer to a heavier harness conformation than that of a harness racer, but they can still be used to improve a wide variety of stock which has also been a part of the Orlov's breeding policy.

Pinto and Paint Horses

The Pinto and the Paint Horse, which have also been known as Calico, are academically color types and only in the U.S.A. do they have breed status. In America these colored horses come under the joint aegis of two societies: the Pinto Horse Association of America and the American Paint Horse Association. Most Paint horses are Pintos, but not all Pintos are Paints!

The Pinto Horse Association of America maintains a register for horses, ponies, and miniatures which is divided into stock type: those with mainly Quarter Horse (page 213) background; Hunter (page 176), largely Thoroughbred (page 122), pleasure, Arab or Morgan; and saddle, based largely on Saddlebred (page126),

Height: Average for horses: 15–16 hh (60-64 in.);
for Pinto ponies, up to 15 hh (60 in.)
Colors: Two patterns for Pinto (Overo and Tobiano), three patterns for Paints (Overo, Tobiano and Tovaro)
Use: Riding, ranch work, trail riding
Features: Varied, see text below

Hackney (page 167) or Tennessee Walking Horse (page 231).

The American Paint Horse Society register places an emphasis on bloodlines rather than simply color or coat pattern: it registers stock-type horses and sets strict standards with regard to conformation, athleticism and temperament. This association requires Paint horses to be

205

registered in one of four recognized associations: the American Paint Quarter Horse Association; the American Paint Stock Horse Association; the Jockey Club; or the American Quarter Horse Association.

Both the Pinto and the Paint descend from the Spanish Horses brought to the New World by the Conquistadors in the 16th century. The name 'Pinto' comes from the Spanish word *pintado* which means 'painted'. In Europe horses with two colors, other than the spotted breeds, are called 'part', or 'odd-colored'. The British further distinguish between coats with patches of black and white – these are called piebald – and those with patches of white and any other color, which are called skewbald. ('Bald' is the old English word for a white-faced horse). In the U.S.A. more precise

terms are used: in the Pinto, coat patterns fall into two types: Overo and Tobiano. In Paint horses, a third 'classification' is used: Tovaro.

Tobiano patterns are the dominant coloring, and are distinguished by a white coat overlaid with any basic color common to horses, such as brown, bay, chestnut, dun, or gray. Tobianos may have head markings like those of solid-colored horses, such as a blaze, strip, star or snip. Generally, all four legs of Tobiano horses are white, at least below the hocks and knees. The spots of color are regular and distinctly oval or round in shape and the tail, although sparse (which is a common trait in spotted horses) is often in two colors.

The Overo pattern is the recessive pattern

in coats. This is a solid coat of color with irregular patches of white. Typically, the white patches on an Overo will not cross the back of the horse between its withers and tail, and generally, all four legs will be dark and the tail will be of one color.

But not all coat patterns fit neatly into the two: the American Paint Horse Association has expanded its classification to include 'Tovaro' which is used to describe a Paint horse with both Overo and Tobiano characteristics. Whatever their color or pattern, no two Pintos or Paints will look identical.

In any case, these distinctive coat markings are not achieved by mating a white horse with another of solid, darker color. Two mono-colored horses will not produce two-colored offspring unless one or both of the parents has the specific spotting genes inherited from a Pinto or Paint ancestor. Breeding two Paint or Pinto horses does not result in a two-colored foal each time, either. Consequently, Pinto and Paint foals can be rare and are extremely desirable.

The Sioux and Crow Indians considered Pinto and Paint horses advantageous not only because their coats provided perfect camouflage, but because they were very tough horses. Cowboys, too, held them in great esteem: many considered these horses to be especially lucky and were willing to pay a higher price for one. A recurring point in the testimony of many wranglers and cattlemen who swore by the supremacy of these horses was their characteristic ruggedness and their incredible ability to survive in the most rigorous of country. Powerful horses with strong bodies and back, robust quarters, a good head and neck, Paints and Pintos are carefully bred to ensure good conformation and correct limbs and feet. Their intelligence also makes them valued for ranch work and rodeos, as well as for pleasure and trail riding, and showing.

Palomino

Height: **14.1–16 hh (56-64 in.)**
Colors: **Light gold with white tail and mane. Any white socks should not extend above the knees.**
Use: **Ranch work, rodeo, pleasure and trail riding**
Features: **Variable height, skin either dark or golden color; no smudges of color on coat; mane and tail white with no more than 15% of darker hairs in either; hazel or dark eyes; white facial markings limited to blaze, snip or star; white socks can extend no higher than knees.**

Like Pintos and Paints, the Palomino is descended from the Spanish Horses brought to North America in the 16th century by the Conquistadors. The origin of the name Palomino are uncertain: some say it is derived from the Spanish *palomilla* which apparently – and conveniently – means a 'cream-colored horse with a white mane and tail'. Others maintain it is derived from *paloma*, the Spanish for dove. In Spain itself, the Palomino coloring is called Ysabella after the queen who encouraged horse-breeding in that color.

The Palomino is a 'color breed' – it is defined by color rather than by conformation – although its physique is usually that of a riding horse. The Palomino is recognized as a breed only in the U.S.A., although they are bred elsewhere. Even in

the U.S.A., because of variations in size and appearance, the Palomino does not have true breed status. It is also quite a different sort of color breed to the Appaloosa (see page 134) or Pintos and Paints (see page 205): the gorgeous golden coat is not the result of a Palomino gene and so it can therefore appear in any breed or strain where the spotted gene has been bred out. The Palomino color can therefore be found in other horse breeds, especially in the Quarter Horse (see page213).

In 1936 the Palomino Horse Association Inc. was founded to perpetuate and improve the horses by recording bloodlines and registering horses which met their stringent 'breed standards'. The height may vary from 14.1–16 hh (56-64 in.), but the color requirement is very specific. The Palomino is a solid-coated horse which, much like any other single-colored horse such as bays and chestnuts, should not have any areas of white at all on the body. The skin must be of an overall uniform color: a dark, grayish black or a golden color. The coat must be no more than three shades lighter or darker than a newly minted gold coin and must be free from smudges. There must be no hint of a dorsal stripe on the back – a usual feature of dun

colored horses, and any zebra marks on the legs (another sign of 'primitive' origins) are also unacceptable in the Palomino. The mane and tail should be white and may contain no more than 15% of darker hairs. The eyes must be hazel or dark: horses of Pinto, Paint, Albino or Appaloosa parentage, which may have pink, blue or wall eyes, are ineligible for inclusion in the Palomino register. White facial markings are also limited to a blaze, snip, or star, and white socks cannot extend above the knees and hocks.

To qualify for entry into the breeding register, stallions and mares must have one parent already in the register, while the other must be Quarter Horse, Arab or Thoroughbred. While color is a prime requirement, the Palomino Horse Association Inc. will not tolerate poor conformation in any horse. The conformation of Palominos is that of the predominant cross: consequently it may tend towards the working stock horse-type, or to the 'finer' parade-type horse.

Because the golden coat color is not the result of a special 'Palomino gene', producing Palomino coloration is not difficult and can be deliberately brought about by at least four known crosses:

209

Palomino to Palomino, which produces an average ratio of two Palomino offspring to one chestnut and one albino offspring; Palomino to chestnut, which produces an average of one chestnut to one Palomino foal. This crossing tends to produce the richest and most dazzling golden color in Palomino coats. The third crossing is Palomino to albino which produces on average, one Palomino to one albino offspring. The fourth crossing, chestnut to albino produces only Palomino foals. While this crossing is the most consistent, it can however, also produce a color that is often flat, dull, and 'washed out'.

The Palomino is in great demand, not only for its good looks, but also for its skill and aptitude in Western riding activities, for ranch and rodeo work, and for pleasure and trail riding.

Peruvian Paso

The Peruvian Paso, also known as the Peruvian Stepping Horse, is the most prominent of the Peruvian horse breeds and shares a common ancestry with the Criollo (see page 148) of Argentina, which is descended from Spanish stock – a mixture of Arab, Barb, and Andalucian brought to America in the 16th century. The first horses were imported to Peru in 1531-32 by Francisco Pizarro, and the Peruvian Paso is descended from these horses. Like the Criollo, the Peruvian Paso is a horse of great stamina: it has excellent bones and very hard feet, as well as relatively large

Height: **14–15 hh (56-60 in.)**
Colors: Bay and chestnut predominate, but all solid colors may be found
Use: Riding
Features: Well muscled, short, upright neck; notable muscled structure in chest; long, strong hind legs with flexible joints; hard feet; quarters are lowered, long mane and tail.

heart and lungs, all of which make it well suited to working at high altitudes in the Andes mountains.

Over the centuries, the Peruvian Paso has been systematically and carefully developed for its characteristic lateral gaits, the *paso llano* and the *paso sobreandando*. Both of these gaits are natural and every pure-bred Peruvian Paso inherits them; training only serves to increase muscular development and flexibility (as well as teaching the horse to respond to riders' cues).

The *paso llano* is the most commonly seen of the two gaits and can be described as a 'smooth walk' which, while similar to the rack of the American Saddlebred (see page 126) or the running walk of the Tennessee Walking Horse (see page 123), and Missouri Fox Trotter (see page 191), in the Peruvian paso, it is marked by characteristically energetic, round, dishing action of the forelegs – an action called *termino* – supported by a very powerful movement of the hind legs overstepping the prints of the forefeet. An even 1-2-3-4 cadence can be heard, with the hind foot striking the ground just before the forefoot. The quarters are noticeably lowered and the back is held straight, level and rigid. The *paso llano* can be maintained at a steady 11 mph (18 km/h) for long periods over the roughest mountain trails and so smooth is the gait that it can reach speeds of 13 mph (21 km/h) without the rider suffering any discomfort whatsoever.

The *sobreandando* maintains the four beat cadence but is a little more of an 'overdrive' and perhaps, a little closer to the pace. In the show ring, judges will often ask for a Peruvian Paso to accelerate or slow down to see the range of speeds that can be achieved while maintaining the pure gait.

Quarter Horse

The Quarter Horse, or to give it its full and correct name, the American Quarter Running Horse, is the oldest all-American horse breed (although the Morgan, which came into being in the 18th century is the oldest documented American breed). The history of the Quarter Horse begins in the early 17th century in Virginia and the other early English colonial settlements on the east coast, where the inhabitants obtained 'native' mares – descendants of the Spanish horses brought earlier by the Spanish explorers – from the Chickasaw Indians which were crossed with imported English 'running horses'. The first import of English horses to Virginia was a cargo of 17 stallions and horses which arrived in 1611. These 'running horses' (which would later provide the basis for the Thoroughbred (see page 122) may have been the now extinct Galloways, swift ponies bred in the north of Britain between Nithsdale and the Mull of Galloway, and Irish Hobbies, a breed of pony found in Connemara in the west of Ireland in the 16th and 17th centuries and also noted for its speed.

The resulting offspring were

Height: **15–16 hh (60-64 in)**
Colors: All solid colors
Use: Riding, racing, ranch work, rodeo
Features: Compact horse with a short head on a muscular, flexible neck; strong shoulders; well defined withers that extend back beyond top of shoulders; underline (belly)is longer than back; short cannons and hocks set low to ground; no play in joint other than directly forwards; oblong hoof with same degree of slope as in pastern, about 45 degrees; heavy muscular quarters

ideally suited to the demands of early colonial life: they performed farm work, hauled goods and lumber at mills, conveyed churchgoing folk in carriages on Sundays, and carried the master astride on a comfortable gait when he went on business. All this on a pretty meager diet supplemented by what the horse could forage for. Compact, and 'chunky' – averaging 15 hh (60 in.) with massive, muscular quarters, these horses had tremendous thrust and pull through the shoulders and haunches. It was this extraordinary power that would lead to the

Quarter Horse becoming the master of the short-distance sprint. The love of racing was not diminished among the English in the New World, and while much of their time was spent building a new land – with little left for building race courses – nevertheless, any main street or clearing of a quarter of a mile in length would suffice as a race track – and would eventually give the breed its name.

The rise of the Thoroughbred and the construction of the now familiar oval-shaped race tracks stimulated interest in long-distance racing so that the original

quarter-mile sprints were eventually abandoned in the eastern seaboard states. When pioneers began moving westward, their efficient and versatile Quarter Horses went west too: its agility and speed made it a favorite cow pony. It is often said that the Quarter Horse could 'Turn on a dime and toss you back nine cents change' from a flat out gallop. Consequently, Quarter Horse racing was kept alive and well in the western states: the top prize in Quarter Horse racing is the All-American Futurity Stakes which are run annually in California and are worth in excess of half a million dollars.

In the 19th century, as the ranches grew in size, and cattle were being selectively bred for increased profitability, ranchers also began upgrading their horse stocks. Some were regrettably more concerned with the performance of their horses than pedigree, and bloodlines became confused. It was only in the early 1900s that the first serious attempts to trace the Quarter Horse's origins were made.

There are 12 principal Quarter Horse families, at the root of which are the breed's two most important foundation sires, Janus, an imported English horse who died in 1780 and was responsible through his son of the same name for the Printer line, and Sir Archy, the son of the first ever English Derby winner Diomed – who was also concerned with the beginnings of the American Saddlebred. The Shiloh, Old Billy, Steel Dust and Cold Deck families trace back to him. Through the diligent research of Robert Denhard, a Quarter Horse enthusiast, the American Quarter Horse Association was formed in 1940. The first horse to be registered was Wimpy, listed as P-1 in the stud book. Today, there are more than three million Quarter Horses registered, making it the largest horse breed organization in the world.

Racking Horse

Height: Average 15.2 hh (61 in.)
Colors: All colors including spotted
Use: Riding, jumping and show ring
Features: Long, sloping neck; well boned; smooth legs; finely textured hair.

The Racking Horse is famous for its beauty, stamina, calm temperament and most of all, for its smooth, easy lateral gait. The Racking Horse has its origins deep in Tennessee Walking Horse (see page 231) bloodlines and until 1971, it did not have a registry or a uniform set of breed rules. In the 1960s a detailed program of research into the breed began and a group of

Alabama business men, headed by Joe D. Bright formed a corporation and initiated the legal process with the Department of Agriculture (U.S.D.A.) to designate the Racking Horse as a distinct breed. In May 1971 the U.S.D.A. recognized the Racking Horse Breeders' Association of America, and allowed a registry to be established. The association chose the name 'racking' so that the new horse breed would not be tied to a specific American state or region, and eligibility for registration was determined by performance of the gaits that were natural to the breed. In the beginning, horses of all ages were registered because of their gait performance. The Racking Horse is considered a 'light' horse, averaging 15.2 hh (61 in.) and weighing around 1,000 pounds. Colors are varied and can be black, bay, sorrel, chestnut, brown, gray, yellow, cremello, buckskin, dun, palomino (see page 208), champagne, roan, and spotted.
The term 'rack' was the country word for the 'single foot' gait. This is performed at great speed with only one foot on the ground at any one time. There is a complete moment of

suspension when all four feet are off the ground between each footfall. The rack is a four-beat bilateral gait – it is neither a pace nor a trot, and comes as naturally to the breed as walking or trotting comes to others. The rack performed by the Racking Horse must not, therefore, be confused with that performed by other breeds because there, the rack is an artificially achieved gait and is the result of specialized training. There is no difference between the gaits performed by the Racking Horse in the show ring and those performed on the bridle path. Racking Horses may be shown under saddle, in hand or in harness, flat shod, or with very little pad.

217

Rhinelander

Also known as: Rheinlander, Rheinish
Height: 16.2 hh (65 in.)
Colors: All solid colors with chestnut predominant
Use: Riding
Features: Plain head on short, thick but strong neck; strong shoulders are reasonable riding type but are heavy and lack depth; clean legs but feet seem small and narrow in relation to large body

The Rhinelander is a relatively new warmblood breed from Germany. Developed in the 1970s, the Rhinelander is based on the old Rheinisch-Deutsches Pferd (Rhenish-German Horse), or Rhineland heavy draught horse which was once a very popular work horse in the Rhineland, Westphalia and Saxony regions. This horse's chief qualities were early maturity, efficient food conversion, and a very good temper. But, with modern agricultural practices, this heavy draught breed became redundant and is no longer recognized in Germany.

The Rhenish Stud Book, however, was never closed, and breeders, using the lighter specimens of the breed, worked towards developing a warmblooded riding horse. Stallions from the Hanover-Westphalia area were used on warmblood mares sired by Thoroughbreds (see page 122), Trakehners (see page 234), and

Hanoverians (see page 169) out of dams which claimed a relationship with the old Rhenish heavy horse breed.

From this mix of blood, the best half-bred stallions were selected to develop the Rhinelander breed. The result is a riding horse about 16.2 hh (65 in.), often chestnut in color. While the early examples lacked bone, breeders continued to concentrate on developing an improved conformation, an even temperament, and the straight action which distinguishes German breeds. The modern Rhinelander may not as yet be as distinguished as the Holsteiner (page 174) or the Hanoverian, but its qualities as a riding horse that is greatly suited to the average (even novice) leisure rider are highly recommended.

Rocky Mountain Horse

Height: 14.2–14.3 hh (57-57.5 in.)

Colors: Chocolate

Use: Riding and harness

Features: Graceful, long neck flaxen mane and tail; excellent feet; strong hind legs; withers are not sharply defined, but back is good;

The Rocky Mountain horse – which was formerly referred to as a pony – is a very distinctive animal. The Rocky Mountain horse is, in fact, a 'breed in the making': its history is less than 20 years old which is not enough time for it to acquire the fixed characteristics of a breed. Nevertheless, a registry was opened in 1986 and there are more than 200 horses registered. Careful and selective breeding will ensure that this very attractive, sure-footed horse with its ambling gait, achieves great success and popularity.

Like many American horses, the origins of the Rocky Mountain Horse lie in the Spanish horses brought to the New World in the 16th century and later Mustang (see page 226) stock. The credit for the modern development of this distinctive horse belongs to Sam Tuttle of Stout Springs, Kentucky, who ran the riding concession at the Natural Bridge State Resort Park. This offered visitors a unique opportunity to ride the rugged trails of the foothills of the Appalachian Mountains. A favorite horse with the visitors was a stallion called Old Tobe, who was famed for his sure-footedness and his comfortable ambling gait (a slow version of the pacing gait) which he had inherited from his distant Spanish ancestors. It may be also that Old Tobe had a genetic relation to the old Narragansett Pacer, a horse that was highly prized by 19th century plantation owners and which would exert a great influence on American gaited horse breeds.

Narragansetts were said to be small horses – no bigger then the Rocky Mountain – smooth-moving, and sure-footed in the most rocky and rugged of terrain. They were also very hardy horses – a quality shared by the Rocky Mountain Horse.

Old Tobe was active on the trails – and on the mares – until he was 37 years old, and he passed on all his fine qualities to his offspring, among whom there were some unusual chocolate-colored foals. This color is not a prerequisite for registration, but it is a much-prized and very attractive attribute, especially when combined with the beautiful flaxen color of the mane and tail. This chocolate color is a little reminiscent of the 'bloodstone' color that is very occasionally found in

Highland Ponies (see page 69), but how it appears in the Rocky Mountain is something of a mystery. There are no records of this color in horses in early Spanish or colonial horses, but the last of the Narragansett Pacers, a mare who died in 1880, was described as being an 'ugly sorrel color'. It is possible that this 'ugly' color somehow became refined over a century.

The Rocky Mountain Horse is currently judged principally on its natural ambling gait, a lateral gait rather than the conventional trot. This can carry the rider very comfortably at a steady 7 mph over rough trails. Where the going is good, speeds of 16 mph can be achieved.

Russian Trotter

Height: 15.3–16 hh (61-64 in.)

Colors: Black, bay, chestnut, gray

Use: Harness racing

Features: Slightly convex head: pronounced muscular development; hard, clean limbs; sound, strong feet; short cannons; quick to mature, reaching full height at 4 years old; action is low and very long.

Trotting is one of the most popular equestrian sports in the countries of the former U.S.S.R., and harness racing horses, like the Orlov Trotter (see page 203) have been bred there since the 18th century. The Russian Trotter is a more recent breed: it has only been recognized as such since 1949. Breeding began in the second half of the 19th century when Russian racers and breeders realized that the Orlov Trotter was being outclassed in international events by the American Standardbred.

The obvious solution was to cross the Orlov with imported Standardbreds. Between 1890 and 1914, 156 stallions and 220 Standardbred mares were imported. Among these were notable horses including General Forrest, who had trotted one mile in 2 minutes and 8 seconds; Bob Douglas (2 minutes 4 seconds), and the reigning world-record holder at the time Creceus, with a mile time of 2 minutes 2 seconds. The resulting offspring were indeed faster, but they were also smaller and less refined than the Orlov, and unlike the Orlov, these horses were not a suitable type for upgrading agricultural horses: the average mare stood around 15.1 hh (61 in.) and had a girth measurement of 5 ft 9 in with a bone measurement below the knee of 7 ½ inches).

A new breeding program of interbreeding the cross-breds was introduced, dedicated to increasing the trotting speed, as well as improving the height, frame, body measurements, and overall conformation of the Russian Trotters.

The modern standard for Russian Trotters calls for stallions to be 16 hh (64 in.) and mares to be 15.3 hh (61 inches). The barrel length is fixed at 5 ft 4 in and the depth of girth is set at 6 ft 1 in for a stallion (and a little less for mares). Below the knee, a bone measurement of 7 ¾ in. is also required.

Initially, efforts were concentrated on producing three distinct types: the 'thick' type with the proportions of a heavy horse; the 'medium' type, a lighter, though still substantial light agricultural horse; and the 'sporting' type, the modern Russian Trotter, which is significantly faster than the Orlov. While the Russian Trotter is quick to mature, and reaches it full height at four years old, optimum trotting speeds are not achieved in the breed until the horse has reached five or even six years old. The breed is kept pure, although in the 1970s and 1980s, further American Standardbreds were imported to improve the speeds. In some strains, however, this has produced a tendency to pace rather than use the diagonal gait.

Selle Français

Height: **15.2 16.3 hh (61-65 in.)**

Colors: **Predominantly chestnut, but all solid colors may be found.**

Use: **Riding, competition**

Features: **Plain head on long, elegant neck; strong, compact body; powerful shoulders but not sufficiently sloped for great galloping; broad quarters; powerful limbs and strong hocks; bone measurement of at least 8 in below the knee; ideally suited to show jumping.**

crossed with imported English Thoroughbred (see page 122) and English half-bred stallions which had a background of the important and robust Norfolk Trotter. The French breeders produced two crossbreds: a fast harness horse which would eventually become the French Trotter, and, the Anglo-Norman, which was subdivided into a draught cob and riding horse. The riding horse was the prototype for the modern Selle Français, an all-round competition horse.

Le Cheval du Selle Français – the French Saddle Horse – is one of number of European warmbloods or 'half-breds', but what is significant about the Selle Français is the use of fast trotting stock. The origins of the Selle Français date back to the early 19th century in the horse-raising districts of Normandy, in northern France. Here the local Norman mares were

Throughout two world wars, French breeders were able to maintain a small stock of Norman mares and after World War II, further crosses were made with French Trotters (page 158), Arabs (page 113), and Thoroughbreds – including the notable stallion Furioso – to develop a quality horse that combined speed, stamina and jumping ability. The appellation Cheval de Selle Français came into use in December 1958 to describe French 'half-bred' competition horses. Before that time, all French riding horses other than Thoroughbreds, Arabs, and Anglo-Arabs were simply known as '*demi-sangs*' ('half-bloods'). Most Selle Français stand over 16 hh (64 in.), but until the 1980s, the breed was officially split into five classifications. There were three medium-weight horses : small (15.3 hh/61in.), medium (up to 16.1 hh/65 in.), and large (over 16.1 hh/65 in.); and two heavy-weights: small (under 16 hh/64 in.) and large (over 16 hh/64 inches). Today, show jumping is now the main specialization of the breed, but a lighter Selle Français (which carries a greater amount of Thoroughbred blood) is bred for racing limited to non-Thoroughbred horses and is known as AQPSA (*Autre que pur-sang Anglais*).

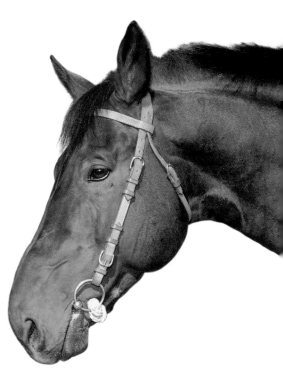

Mustangs: Spanish and Suffield

Height: About 14 hh (56 in.)

Colors: All colors including appaloosa and zebra striped dun, grulla (slate gray) buckskin (ranges from light cream to dark brown), roan, paint, ysabella, palomino, cremello and perlino. All color patterns accepted except Tobiano.

Use: Riding

Features: Spanish type head with straight or convex profile; necks are quite well crested in mares and geldings, heavily crested in stallions; chests are narrow but deep, with front legs joining chest in an 'A' shape rather than straight across; short back; low withers; sloping croup; low set tails; 'mule feet' – concave sole which resists bruising; short canons, but a larger circumference than other breeds of comparable size and height; upper foreleg is long. Many are gaited.

The term 'mustang' is derived from the Spanish word *mestena* which means a group or herd of wild horses. The Mustang is descended from Spanish stock introduced by the Conquistadors in the 16th century and was an important influence on a large number of American breeds. Mustangs come in all types of build, shapes, sizes and colors. The average size is about 14.2 hh (57 in.) but it is not uncommon to see shorter or taller examples. The most often seen colors are sorrel and bay, but any color – and coat pattern including spotted and paint – is possible.

A number of Spanish horses either escaped or were turned loose and became feral and formed the nucleus of the once-great herds of wild horses that spread up from Central America into the western plains of the United States. At the beginning of the 20th century there were an estimated one million wild horses roaming the U.S.A. By 1970, however, their numbers had dramatically fallen as the result of wholesale massacres for the meat market and fewer than 17,000 horses remained.

During the 1950s, in Nevada, Velma B. Johnston, later known as 'Wild Horse Annie' became aware of the ruthless manner in which these horses were being 'harvested' for commercial purposes. She led a grassroots campaign that brought the issue to public attention. The outrage that followed eventually led to a bill passed in 1959 (known as the 'Wild Horse Annie Act') which prohibited the use of motorized vehicles to hunt horses and burros on all public lands. Regrettably, the law did not initiate a government program to protect, manage and control the wild stock.

In the 1950s and 1960s, anxious to preserve their wild horse heritage, a number of enthusiasts formed societies to preserve, manage and improve Mustang stocks. These included the North American Mustang Association and Registry, and the Spanish Barb Breeders' Association. In 1971, the Mustang was declared an endangered species and was protected by law under the Wild Free-Roaming Horse and Burro Act. According to the U.S. Bureau of Land Management (BLM) there are approximately 48,624 Mustangs living in ten western states today.

There are now numerous groups which are involved in research and protection, such as the International Society for the Protection of the Mustang and Burros, the Wild Horse Organised Assistance; the National Mustang Group, and the National Wild Horse Association.

Spanish Mustangs

The first Mustang 'support group' was founded by Mustang breeder Robert E. Brislawn of Oshoto, Wyoming, in 1957. This was the Spanish Mustang Registry which aimed to preserve the purest possible strains of early Spanish horses of both Barb and Andalucian type. Brislawn had in fact started his preservation project in 1925 with

two full brothers called Buckshot and Ute, who had been sired by a Buckskin stallion named Monty out of a Ute reservation mare. Monty was captured in 1927 in Utah. Within every Mustang herd is a dominant stallion who is the leader of at least one mare or a group of mares. Among the mares there is also one dominant horse who leads the herd to graze, to water and to shelter, while the dominant stallion follows up in the rear, protecting his herd from intrusions by other stallions. Mustangs bond with each other within the herd, so when Monty escaped back to the wild in 1944, he also took his mares with him, and he was never recaptured.

In spite of this setback, Brislawn continued in his efforts, collecting individual horses he considered to be the best examples of the breed. Brislawn was looking for a small horse of about 14 hh (56 in.) and weighing about 800 lb, short in the back, low in the withers and with a low sloping croup. In 1957, 20 horses were registered; by 2001, the Spanish Mustang Registry contained 3,000 Spanish Mustangs. While it is still considered a rare breed by the American Rare Breeds Conservancy, the Spanish Mustang's future looks as bright as the horses are colorful. The Spanish Mustang is a medium-sized horse averaging around 14 hh (56 in.) with a proportional weight. They are smooth muscled and short-backed, with rounded rumps and low-set tails. Long-strided, many Spanish Mustangs are gaited with a comfortable four-beat gait such as the 'single foot' or amble. Some are laterally gaited and can perform a 'paso' gait (see Peruvian Paso, page 211) but without the extreme knee action.

Because of their short backs, powerful quarters, and 'bruise resistant' hard feet, Spanish Mustangs are ideally suited to endurance and trail riding and can also do very well at advanced dressage movement. With their energy and precise footwork, they are popular as polo-playing ponies, while their sensible characters also make them ideal pony club mounts.

Suffield Mustangs

The Suffield Mustang is a bloodline that has developed from domesticated stock that was subject to decades of natural selection. Some 1,200 horses, divided into small herds with a stallion at the head, moved freely across one of the largest areas of natural prairie in southern Alberta, Canada, until the military annexed the rangelands in 1941.

Throughout the 1950s and early 1960s, the wild horses on the Canadian Forces base at Suffield were loosely managed by the local ranchers and among the wild horses, some Thoroughbreds (see page 122) Quarter Horses (see page 213), Morgans (see page 195), and Arabs (see page 113) were also turned out. In 1965 the military fenced off the Suffield base, effectively cutting off access by the local ranchers to the horses, which now had to survive unmanaged by humans. From what started out as high quality stock, through interbreeding, and the process of natural selection, a horse of superb quality evolved.

But the Suffield Mustangs' ability to adapt, survive, and reproduce on the open range, nearly caused their downfall: in the early 1990s the military authorities decided that the herds were damaging the grasses on the base and the number of horses needed to be controlled. In 1994 it was decided to round up the Mustangs and to disperse them to anyone willing to take one. Those people who had the foresight to recognize the historical importance of these horses, adopted a Suffield Mustang and joined together to form the Suffield Mustang Association of Canada with the aim to promote and preserve the bloodlines. Around 200 horses from the original 1,200 horses were registered as foundation stock and since 1994, 350 Suffield Mustang foals have been added to the register.

Tennessee Walking Horse

One of the most popular breeds in America, the Tennessee Walking Horse, or Tennessee Walker, was once also called a 'Turn-Row' horse because it was used to inspect the crops on the plantations of 19th century Tennessee, Kentucky, and Missouri, in rows. Speed was not important, but a strong and stylish horse that provided a very comfortable ride for the plantation owner through the fields was.

Like all the American gaited horse breeds, the Tennessee Walking Horse is descended from the old Narragansett Pacer of Rhode Island with later additional input from Thoroughbreds (page 122), Standardbreds (page 128), and Morgans (page 195). The most important influence on refining the previously quite stocky Walker was made in 1914 with the infusion of American Saddlebred (page 126) blood, introduced by Giovanni, who stood at Wartrace in Tennessee.

In 1935 the Tennessee Walking Horse Breeders' Association was formed at Lewisburg, Tennessee which promised 'Ride one today, you'll own one tomorrow'. In 1947, the breed was officially recognized by the U.S. Department of Agriculture.

The modern Tennessee Walking Horse is deep-bodied and short-coupled, with a

Height: 15–16 hh (60-64 in.)
Colors: Black, bay, chestnut as well as part-colored
Use: Riding, show ring
Features: Quite large head carried low; large boned, deep and short-coupled with a square look to the barrel; clean, strong quarters legs; shoeing is critical to the unique pace: foot is grown long and fitted with shoes to give lift to the action; tail is set high, grown long and is usually nicked (according to U.S. conventions).

head that tends to be plain and is carried much lower than the saddlebred. The Tennessee Walker also moves with a much less elevated action. Primarily a show and pleasure riding horse, the Tennessee Walker is famous for two things. First, its steady and reliable temperament which makes it the ideal mount for even the most inexperienced novice rider. Second, the breed's soft, gliding gait which is virtually bounce-free and said to be the most comfortable ride in the world – an added bonus for first timers in the saddle.

The Tennessee Walking Horse has three gaits: the flat walk, the running walk (which is the predominant gait) and the rolling 'rocking-chair' canter marked by the horse's head nodding in a distinctive

manner. Both of the walks are in four-beat time, with each foot hitting the ground separately at regular intervals. In the running walk, the hind feet overstep the print of the front feet by between 6 and 15 inches. The result is a very smooth gliding motion accompanied by the nodding head – and at top speeds of 15 mph over short distances – and by clicking teeth as well.

The gliding movement is accentuated by the elongated heels on the hind shoes. The front feet are also grown long and fitted with shoes that give lift to the action. While these may make the Walker's feet look 'artificial' they do not injure the horse in any way and rarely does the Tennessee Walker suffer from any tendon problems.

Tersky

This elegant and athletic Russian horse was developed between 1921 and 1950 at the Tersk and Stavropol Studs in the northern Caucasus as a deliberate attempt to preserve the old Strelets Arab which had nearly died out. The Strelets was an Anglo-Arab rather than a pure-bred Arabian, the result of crossing pure-breds with Anglos from the Orlov and Rastopchin Studs. By the end of World War I only two Strelets stallions, Cylinder and Tsenitel had survived and both were the characteristic light-gray color with a silvery sheen. But with no Strelets available to attempt pure-breeding, crossing with Arabs and cross-bred Don/Arab and Strelets/Kabardin began and the resulting offspring were carefully chosen for conformation. After 30 years of selective work, the type was sufficiently fixed for the new Tersky breed to be recognized.

The modern Tersky are distinctly Arab in appearance, although they are a little larger and heavier in build. They are characterized by a particularly light, elegant movement. Most are gray with a silver sheen, or white, often with a rosy sheen which is imparted by the pink skin beneath the coat. Immensely popular in circuses, they are also excellent jumpers and strong cross-country horses.

Height: **15 hh (60 in.)**
Colors: **Silver-gray, white**
Use: **Riding**
Features: **Head is of Arab-type with large eyes and straight profile; short back, deep chest, well sprung ribs; legs are clean and there is 7 ½ in of bone below knee; feet are rounded; mane and tail are usually short and thin, hair is very fine and tail is carried high.**

Trakehner

Height: **16–16.2 hh (64-65 in.)**

Colors: **All solid colors**

Use: **Riding, competition**

Features: **'Noble' head on long elegant neck; alert, mobile ears; width between very expressive eyes; good, well-shaped shoulders; powerful quarters; medium-long body, well-ribbed; good, strong limbs and hard hooves. Overall conformation is like a Thoroughbred of substance.**

The Trakehner, also known as the East Prussian, is an ancient breed, based on the Schwieken and dating from the 13th century. In the area between Gumbinnen and Stalluponen (now in present-day Poland), the Teutonic Knights established a horse breeding industry using the Schwieken as its base. This horse was much used in farming and, as a descendent of the Tarpan, was a very strong and hardy horse. Using these horses, the Knights developed strong cavalry horses that carried them to the crusades. In 1732, Frederick William I of Prussia ordered the marshes drained and the Royal Trakehner Stud Administration was established. This was the main source of stallions for all Prussia and the area soon established a reputation for breeding elegant and fast, coach horses.

By 1787 the emphasis had shifted to breeding cavalry remounts and chargers, as well as horses which were capable of being used for agricultural work. The type of horse was developed at the beginning of the 19th century was an out-cross of Arabs (see page 113), but later, increasing numbers of English Thoroughbreds (see page 122) were used. Two of the most influential Thoroughbreds were Perfectionist (son of the winner of the 1896 Epsom Derby and St Leger, Persimmon, who was owned and bred by King Edward VII of England), and Tempelhuter (Perfectionist's son). Their blood appears in nearly all modern Trakehner pedigrees. Although by 1913, nearly all Trakehner stallions were Thoroughbred, Arab content, always remained a powerful balancing agent in the breed in order to offset any deficiencies in either constitution or temperament caused by the Thoroughbred.

In order to guarantee the highest possible performance, only stallions that had been subjected to a year's training were used, and before going to stud, they had to be examined at the stallion testing center at Zwion. Among all the warmbloods, the modern Trakehner is probably closest to the 'ideal' of the modern competition horse: in 1936 it dominated in the Berlin Olympics, winning every medal. After World War II, when Germany retreated from Poland, some 1,200 of the 25,000 horses registered in the Trakehner Stud Book reached West Germany after a three-month trek. There are four distinct breeding centers in Germany at Hunnesruck, Rantzau, Schmoel, and Birkhausen with breeding administered by the Society of Breeders and Friends of the Warm Blood Horse of the Trakehner Origin in Hamburg. In Poland, the Trakehner's influence is still top be found in the Wielkopolski.

Russian Trakehner

Height: 16–16.2 hh (64-65 in.)

Colors: All solid colors

Use: Riding, competition

Features: Shares the same characteristics as its European cousin but is a little rangier and lighter: a noble head on long elegant neck; alert, mobile ears; width between very expressive eyes; good, well shaped shoulders; powerful quarters; medium-long body, well ribbed; good, strong limbs and hard hooves. Overall conformation is like a Thoroughbred of substance.

The Russian Trakehner shares the same origins as its European cousin the Trakehner (see page 234), but it is a slightly rangier and lighter horse, that is very popular in Russia as a competition horse where it is raced on the flat and over hurdles. Trakehners first arrived in Russia in 1925 from what was then East Prussia. Most of these horses were used as remounts for the Russian cavalry. A second group arrived at the end of World War II: in October 1944 as the war was reaching its closing stages and the Soviet forces were closing in on the Trakehner Stud, about 800 horses were evacuated by rail and by foot.

They did not travel far enough west and eventually fell into the hands of the Russian occupation forces in Poland and were subsequently shipped to the U.S.S.R. These were concentrated on the Kirov Stud on the Don River and in 1947, the first volume (of seven) of the Russian Trakehner Stud Book was opened by the Russian Institute of Horse Breeding. Although the bulk of breeding still takes place at the Kirov Stud, since the break-up of the former Soviet Union, many Russian Trakehners are bred elsewhere at private studs, the largest of which is the Oros-L, near Kaluga, some 200 km from Moscow.

Ukranian Riding Horse

Height: 16–16. 2 hh (64-65 in.)
Colors: Bay, chestnut, brown
Use: Riding, competition
Features: Straight, long neck; prominent withers;
long, flat back; solid, heavy body

Arctic Russia may well have been the first area in which horses were domesticated: the 'relic' horse of the Ice Age, Przewalski's Stallion still exists in a wild state on the Eastern frontier. Horses have been bred in Russia and its neighboring states for generations, with an emphasis placed on using local breeds particularly suited to the needs and the land of each region.

The Ukrainian Riding Horse is highly regarded in its homeland. Development of the Riding Horse began in the Ukraine after World War II by crossing Nonius (page 197), Furioso-Northstar (page 162), and Gidran mares from Hungary with Thoroughbred (page 122), Trakehner, and Hanoverian (page 169) stallions. Particular value was placed on individuals with a trace of Russian Saddle Horse blood, however. Breeding began at the Ukrainian stud at Dnepropetrovsk and later at the Aleksandriisk, Derkulsk, and Yagolnitsk studs where, to produce quality sports riding horses, pure breeding with corrective crossings with Thoroughbreds was undertaken. The most common colors in the Ukrainian Riding Horse are bay, chestnut, and brown.

The Ukrainian Riding Horse is a large, heavy saddle horse with a solid build, that performs well in events such as dressage: CIS (Commonwealth of Independent States) equestrians riding Ukrainians have been repeatedly highly placed in international competitions including the Olympic Games, the World and European Championships.

Windsor Greys

At the Royal Mews in London there are about 30 horses: the Bays (most of which are Cleveland Bays, although there are some Dutch Bay horses as well) and the Windsor Greys, which are the only horses used to draw the monarch's carriage. These gray horses, which are almost identical, are not a particular breed.

They are called Windsor Greys because, since before Queen Victoria's reign (1837-1901) they were always kept at Windsor Castle until, in the early 20th century, they were moved to the Royal Mews in London by King George V (1910-36).

The Windsor Greys wear the most opulent of the eight sets of state harness when they draw the State Coach. Made of red morocco, each harness weighs 110 lb and is richly ornamented with gold ormolu. The current harnesses were made in 1834 to replace sets made in 1762. By tradition, the manes of the 'state horses' are always plaited: Bays wear scarlet ribbons, while Windsor Greys wear purple ribbons with a matching brow band and rosette forming part of the bridle.

Buckskins

Like the Windsor Grey, Cremello (see page 241), and Palomino (see page 208), Buckskins are a 'color' and can be found in all breed types. The Buckskin horse's color is an indication of its ancestry: in the western states of America, the Buckskins, as well as dun, red dun, and grulla colors, trace back to the Mustangs (see page 226), the descendants of the Spanish Horses which were brought to the New World in the 16th century with the Spanish explorers. Other Buckskins can trace back to the Norwegian Dun, relatives of the primitive Tarpan horse.

There are societies dedicated to preserving particular strains, such as the American Buckskin Registry Association and the International Buckskin Horse Association. They maintain registries and work to preserve and promote these horses. Eligibility is based on color: horses must be either buckskin, dun, grulla, red dun, or brindle dun.

Buckskin-colored horses have a body coat which is a shade of tan, but that can range from very light (called 'creme') to very dark (called 'bronze'). The points — the mane, tail, ears and legs — are black or brown, and overall, the buckskin is clean of any 'smuttiness' in color. The guard hairs which are buckskin color, grow through the body coat, up and over, the base of the mane and tail.

Brindle dun is buckskin with a dun factor. This is a buckskin-colored horse but with a dorsal stripe, leg barring, ear 'frames', shoulder stripes, face masking and 'cob webbing' in a 'dirty black' or 'smutty brown' color. Brindle dun horses show up in the Netherlands and are referred to as 'ancient dun color'. The peculiar body markings can appear in the form of tear drops, or as zebra stripes.

Dun is an intense color, but is generally a 'duller' shade than buckskin and may have a more 'smutty' appearance. Most dun horses have dark points of brown or black, and have a dorsal stripe along with shoulder stripes and leg bars.

Red dun can range from 'peach' to 'copper' to 'rich red' but in all shades, the accompanying points will be a darker red or chestnut and contrast with the lighter body color. The dorsal stripe will usually be dark red and very evident.

Grulla (pronounced 'grew-ya') is the rarest of all horse body coat colors. The word 'grulla' is Spanish for crane or heron and like this bird, grulla is a slate color which ranges from bluish-gray to a brownish color, but there are no white hairs mixed in the body hairs. A dorsal stripe, shoulder stripes, and leg barring, in a dark-sepia to black, are also registry requirements in this color.

Cremello

Cremello horses, like Windsor Greys, are not strictly a breed, but a color type. This means that the color can appear in a number of horse breeds.

The color of Cremello horses is the result of the complexities of genetics. Cremellos are 'double diluted' – they have two copies of the cream color gene rather than one. A Palomino (see page 208) gets its color from the fact that it has a single dilution of the basic red (chestnut or sorrel) base color because it inherited one cream gene from one parent. The buckskin color likewise, is a single dilution of the basic bay color.

The Cremello has a double dilution of the cream gene on the red (chestnut or sorrel) base, because it inherited two cream genes – one from each parent. The resulting Cremello color is a rich cream set off by a very pale white mane and tail. Underneath, the skin is a dark pink color all over, while the eyes are blue. Most of the major registries accept Cremello – and Perlino, which is a creamy color but with a darker mane and tail with tan, yellow, or orange hues – except for the American Quarter Horse Association. As the rules currently stand, Cremello (and Perlino) horses cannot be registered with the AQHA – even if both its parents are registered. They can, however, be registered with the American Paint Horse Association as breeding stock.

Miniature Horses

Height: In U.K. (British Miniature Horse Society) not exceeding 34 in.; in USA: not exceeding 34 in. for A.M.H.A. (American Miniature Horse Association). A.M.H.R. (American Miniature Horse Registry) registers 'minis' in two divisions: 'A' Division: 34 in. and under; 'B' Division 34 in. and up to 38 inches.

Colors: All colors

Use: Showing, companion

Features: Miniature horses must possess the correct conformation that is required in other horse breeds, notably, symmetry, strength, agility, alertness. They are to be perfectly formed horses in miniature.

Small horses are usually the product of a harsh natural environment: scarce supplies of food, difficult terrain and severe weather has contributed over the centuries to 'modifying' their stature to enable them to survive. With an understanding of genetics, however, it is possible to selectively breed for particular characteristics such as size – either small, or indeed, very big.

The first true miniature horses originated in Europe and as early at the 17th century, they were bred as pets for the nobility, and for their curiosity value. Lady Estella Hope and her sisters continued breeding the English lines into the mid-19th century, and many of the Miniatures in America are descended from the 'Hope' line. Perhaps the best known of the miniature breeds is the Falabella (see page 63) which, in spite of its size, it not a pony but a true horse, sharing a horse's characteristics and proportions.

Miniature horses are really a 'height breed': the features of Miniature horses are exactly the same as large-size horses: Miniature horses are 'scaled down' versions standing no taller than 34 in. at maturity. They must be healthy, sound, well-balanced, and possess the correct conformation characteristics required of most breeds: the head must be in proportion to the length of the neck and the body; a straight or slightly concave profile; an even bite; a flexible neck blending into the withers; long, sloping shoulders; well muscled forearms.

There should be ample bone and substance to the body, neither overweight or artificially thin; a short back in relation to the underline; smooth and generally level top line; long well-muscled hip, thigh and gaskin; highest point of croup the same height as the withers; smooth rounding at the rump and the tail set neither excessively high or too low.

Legs are set straight and parallel when seen from the back, hooves pointing directly forwards; pasterns slope about 45 degrees and blending smoothly. Hooves should be rounded and there should be a fluid gait in motion. Any color or marking is permissible: the hair is notably silky and lustrous.

Their small size and gentle, affectionate nature makes Miniature horses excellent companions. While they should never be ridden, they are adept at learning to drive and can often to be seen in performance classes at shows where their strength and natural athleticism delights the crowds. They take part in a range of classes, from hunter jumper to showmanship and driving.

British Warmblood

The term 'warmblood' is a relatively recent addition to British breeders vocabulary.

'Cold blood' is used to describe the heavy draught horses such as the Suffolk Punch (see page 104), while 'pure blood' or 'hot blood' is used for the Thoroughbred (see page 122) and Arab (see page 113) horse. Consequently, any horse 'in-between' could be called a warmblood, as they are in Continental Europe. Because Britain had a tradition of hunting on horseback, these 'warmblood in-betweens' were termed Hunters. In Europe, however, which did not have the same hunting tradition, a catch-all term like 'warmblood' was needed to describe the many breeds of driving and riding horses being bred. There is, however, a significant difference between Hunters and Warmbloods: the studbook registration and the selective breeding process.

Nearly every European country imported English-bred carriage and riding horses as foundations for their warmblood breeds: the French developed the Anglo-Norman – the forerunner of their champion warmblood, the Selle Français (page 224) with Norfolk Trotters and Thoroughbreds, while most German warmbloods (except the Trakehner) are descended through Hanoverians and Holsteiners from the Yorkshire Coach Horses and Norfolk Trotters of the 19th century. Unlike in Britain, where they were kept for the 'best breeds', on the Continent, breeders were careful to maintain detailed stud books which allowed them to selectively breed different types of horses for different uses. This proved particularly useful when, after the Second World War, mechanization took over from heavy horses in farming, and the demand for leisure and riding horses increased.

Meanwhile, in Britain breeders

were basically breeding for the hunt field and the show ring and were unfamiliar with producing 'performance' or 'competition horses'. However, recently, British breeders have turned their attention to producing a British Warmblood. In many ways, the British can claim an advantage over their continental cousins: by importing foreign-bred stallions they will have the benefits of the same 'hybrid' effect just as much as they did in the past – and the British can

pick and choose the stallions they think are the most useful. In effect, the British are able to reimport their own bloodlines in a more advanced formula. There is also the open and continuous grading system which makes for rapid improvement so it won't be very long before a British Warmblood will be competing alongside European Warmbloods at international-level competition.

American Warmblood

In Europe, the breeding of warmblood horses for work, sport and driving, has been a very organized undertaking, with breeding strictly controlled by government or federal rules which resulted in horses of extremely high quality. From the 1950s, European warmbloods started arriving in the U.S.A., with more established breeds such as the Swedish Warmblood (page 155), the Bavarian Warmblood (page 138), and the Dutch Warmblood (page 151) finding early acceptance. There is now an American branch of almost every European warmblood breed.

But while the European breeders offered breeding guidelines, they did not consider the American groups to be part of their regional breeding programs: if the 'American' horses are exported to Europe, they would have to be re-examined extensively before they would be allowed into the local breeding population. Since American breeders do not have the requisite allegiance to a specific European country, American breeders contend that all the European warmbloods are 'intermingled' – they are all from one big gene pool – and in

American eyes, they do not represent distinct breeds, but rather, various different types of the Warmblood breed.

By the 1970s many Americans thought that the time had come for them to produce and promote their own sport horse, the American Warmblood. America already possesses a number of elegant and athletic horses that are also graced with agreeable temperaments and fluid gaits which allowed them to excel in competition. In 1981, the American Warmblood Registry was established, and since then it has registered not only European imports, but their American offspring as well an on an equal footing.

Irish Sport Horse

when a number are selected for performance testing. This is done either through open competition, or through central testing. In open competition, the stallions are reassessed at four years and older, while in central testing, they undergo rigorous testing over an intense 12-week period from September to November.

Mares are likewise inspected to be considered for premium status.

The Irish Sport Horse is essentially a cross between a Thoroughbred (page 122) and an Irish Draught Horse (page 175). The Thoroughbred-Irish Draught cross has for a long time been used to produce some of the finest Irish Hunters, but it has been further developed with the aim of producing a warmblood that was particularly suited to show jumping, eventing and dressage, and the combination of the blood produces horses of exceptional soundness, stamina, and temperament.

The breeding program requires that three-year-old stallions are inspected in spring

Canadian Horse

Also known as: Canadian Sports Horse

Height: 14–16 hh (56–60 in.)

Colors: Black predominates, but browns, bays and chestnuts are also common

Use: Riding, harness, competition, ranch work, trail riding

Features: Strong, arched neck; high, well sloping shoulders; long, deep body; rounded barrel; tail set high on powerful rump; mane and tail are long, thick and usually wavy; strong legs and feet.

Known affectionately as the 'Little Iron Horse', the Canadian Horse played a vital role in building the nation. Although listed as 'critical' by the American Livestock Breeds Conservancy with approximately 2,500 head mostly located in Eastern Canada, there has been a great deal of renewed interest in this once very popular breed.

The Canadian Horse traces its origins back to the royal stables of the French King Louis XIV: three shipments were sent from France to the New World: the first, in 1665 consisted of two stallions and 20 mares; the second, in 1667, around 14 horses were sent; and in 1670, a stallion and 11 mares made the transatlantic crossing.

These horses were of Breton and Norman descent – the latter carrying Andalucian (page 130) blood which would manifest itself in the Canadian's trotting ability. It is also possible that there was Friesian (page 160) influence in the feathered legs and magnificent mane and tails, as well as, Arab (page 113) and Barb blood.

The 1670 shipment of horses from France was the last: the colonial governor, Intendant Talon now believed there were enough horses in the colony to supply a regular number of colts for the population. The breeding progam that followed was very successful: by 1679 there were 145 horses in the colony, and by 1698, there were 684.

The Canadian Horse worked the land, provided transport, and entertainment in the form of racing. They endured the freezing winters and the blazing summers on little feed. Famed for their hardiness and stamina, they survived the rigors of life in Canada. But they did become smaller in size – hence their name 'Little Iron Horse' – and produced both trotters and pacers. Consequently, the Canadian Horse was popular in the United States where they contributed to the foundation stock of many American breeds. The demand for Canadian Horses was so great that in fact, by the end of the 19th century, the number of pure Canadians at home had decreased that the breed was in danger of extinction. In 1895 the Canadian Horse Breeders' Association was formed, but even by 1976, the breed was still struggling with only 383 registered Canadian Horses. Thanks to the efforts of a number of dedicated breeders, numbers began the slow climb back from virtual extinction.

The Canadian Horse is a very versatile horse: they are willing and adaptable and have a very even temperament. These qualities, combined with their good looks, have made the Canadian Horse a popular mount for both pleasure riding (their tough legs and hard feet make them very sure-footed trail-riding horses) as well as in harness, as show jumpers and in the dressage ring.

Glossary

Action The movement of the horse's body frame and legs at all paces,

Amble The slow form of the lateral pacing gait,

Barrel The body between the forearms and the loins,

Blood weed A lightly built, poor quality Thoroughbred horse which lacks bone and substance,

Blue feet Dense blue-black coloring of the horn,

Bone The measurement around the leg just below the knee or hock. The bone measurement determines the horse's ability to carry weight.

Breed An equine group bred selectively for consistent characteristics over a long period, whose pedigrees are registered in a stud book.

By A horse is said to be 'by' a particular sire. A horse is said to be 'out of' a mare.

Cannon bone The bone of the foreleg between the knee and fetlock. Also called the 'shin bone'. The corresponding bone in the hind leg is called the shank.

Carriage horse A light, elegant horse used for private or hackney carriage use.

Cavalry remount Also called a 'trooper', a horse used for military service.

Charger Military officer's mount.

Clean-bred A horse of any breed of pure pedigree blood.

Clean-legged Without feather on the lower limbs.

Close-coupled Short back without a hand's width between the last rib and the point of the hip, with no slackness in the loins. Also called short-coupled.

Coach horse A strong, powerfully built horse able to pull a coach.

Cold blood The name for heavy European breeds descended from the prehistoric Forest Horse.

Conformation The way the horse is 'put together' – the shape and proportions of its body.

Cow hocks Hocks that turn inward at the points, like those of a cow.

Cross-breeding Mating individual horses of different breeds or types.

Dam A horse's mother.

Depth of girth The measurement from the wither to the elbow: 'good depth of girth' describes generous measurements between these two points.

Desert Horse A term used to describe horses bred in desert conditions, or horsesbred from desert stock. Such horses are heat-tolerant and can survive on minimal water intake.

Dished face The concave head profile as exemplified by the Arab horse.

Docking Amputation of the tail purely for appearance. Illegal in the UK.

Dorsal stripe A continuous strip of black, brown. or dun-colored hair extending from the neck to the tail. It is a feature of horses with a primitive connection and is most usually found in dun colored horses. Also called an 'eel stripe'.

Draft A word used to describe a horse which draws any vehicle, but generally applied to the heavy breeds.

Dry A word used to describe the 'lean' appearance of the head of desert-bred horses. There is little fatty tissues and the veins stand out clearly under the skin.

Feather Long hair on the lower legs and fetlocks.

Floating The word used to describe the action of the Arab horse's trotting gait.

Forearm The upper part of the front leg, above the knee.

Forelock The mane between the ears which hangs over the forehead.

Gaited horse The American term for horses schooled to artificial as well as natural gaits.

Gaskin The second thigh extending from stifle to hock.

Girth The circumference of the body measured from behind the withers around the barrel.

Hands Height of horses in the U.K. and U.S.A. is measured in 'hands': 1 hand equals 4 inches.

Harness The equipment of a driving horse.

Harness horse A horse used in harness, or with a harness-type conformation: straight shoulders and with an elevated 'harness action'

Haute école The classical art of advanced horsemanship.

Heavy Horse A large draft horse.

Hock The joint in the hind leg between the gaskin and cannon bone – the equivalent of the human ankle.

'Hocks well let down' Where a horse has short cannon bones, considered to give great strength. Long cannons are regarded as a conformational weakness.

Hogged mane The mane clipped close to the neck.

Hot blood Used to describe Arab, Barbs, and Thoroughbreds.

Hybrid A cross between a horse on one side and a zebra or ass, etc., on the other.

Inbreeding Literally incest, e.g. the mating of a sire to a daughter, or dam to a son, or brother to a sister, in order to enhance or fix characteristics.

251

In hand When a horse is controlled from the ground, rather than from the saddle.

Jibbah The bulged formation on the forehead of an Arab horse.

Light Horse A horse other than a heavy horse or pony suitable for riding and carriage work.

Line breeding Mating individual horses which share a common ancestor some generations removed.

Loins The area on either side of the back bone just behind the saddle.

Mitbah Used to describe the angle at which the neck of an Arab horse enters the head. It gives an arched set to the neck and allows for almost all-round movement.

Native ponies Another name for British Mountain and Moorland breeds.

Oriental horses A term that is loosely applied to horses of eastern origin – either Arab or Barb – which were used in the formation of English Thoroughbreds.

Out-crossing Mating unrelated horses; introducing outside blood to the breed

Paces The walk, trot, canter and gallop.

Pacer A horse that uses a lateral action at trot rather than the more conventional diagonal movement: i.e. near fore and near hind leg together followed by the offside pair.

Pack horse A horse used to transport goods in packs carried on either side of its back

Palfrey A medieval light saddle horse that could amble.

Parietal bones The bones on top of the skull.

Part-bred The offspring of a Thoroughbred and another breed.

Pedigree Details of a horse's ancestry recorded in a stud book.

Piebald The British term for a body color of black with white patches.

Points The various parts of the horse's body comprising its conformation. Also used in color description: the mane, tail, legs varying in color from the rest of the body.

Prepotent Able to pass on a character or fixed type to offspring.

Primitive A term used to describe the early subspecies of horses: the Asiatic Wild Horse, the Tarpan, the Forest Horse, and the Tundra Horse.

Pure-bred A horse of unmixed breeding.

Quarters The body from behind the flank to the tail and down to the top of the gaskin.

Ram head A convex profile like that of the Barb, similar to the 'Roman nose' that is found in Shire and other heavy horse breeds.

Rangy A horse with size and scope of movement.

Riding Horse Also called a Saddle Horse. A horse with the conformation associated with a comfortable riding action, as opposed to a draft or carriage horse.

Roached mane The U.S. term for a hogged mane.

Running Horse The English racing stock, also called Running Stock, which provided the base for the English Thoroughbred when crossed with   imported Oriental sires.

Second thigh Gaskin.

Shoulders The angle from the point of the shoulder to the withers should be 45 degrees in a riding horse. If the shoulder or the pastern is too upright, the horse's action will not be smooth and comfortable.

Skewbald The British term for a body color of irregular white and colored patches other than black.

Slab-sided Flat-ribbed.

Stud A breeding establishment. Also a stallion (an uncastrated male horse of four years old or more).

Stud book The book kept by a breed society in which the pedigrees of stock eligible for entry are recorded.

Top line The line of the back from the withers to the end of the croup.

Type A horse that fulfils a particular purpose, such as a cob, hunter or hack, but which does not belong to a specific breed.

Warmblood In general terms, a half-, or part-bred horse, the result of an Arab or Thoroughbred cross with other blood or bloods.

Well-ribbed A short, deep, rounded body with well-sprung ribs which gives ample room for lung expansion and is suitable for carrying a saddle.

Withers The part of the horse where the neck joins the body.

Zebra bars Dark, striped markings on the forearms and sometimes on the hind legs.

253

Index

Bibliography:

Elwyn Hartley Edwards *The New Encyclopedia of the Horse* (Dorling Kindersley, 2000)

Elwyn Hartley Edwards *Ultimate Horse* (Dorling Kindersley, 2002)

Elizabeth Peplow (ed) *Encyclopedia of the Horse* (Hamlyn, 2002)

Collins Gem Horses and Ponies (Harper Collins, 1999)

Horse & Hound magazine

If you want to learn more about your favorite horse breed, log onto the internet and check out the various breed clubs and societies and click on the links to other sites to find out more.

Acknowledgments:

Vic Swift at the British Library, London, but special thanks to all the breed societies and associations, and to all the horse enthusiasts, around the world, who willingly shared their expert knowledge of breeds, history, types, colors, and features on the internet.

Addresses:

The American Association of Riding Schools
8375 Coldwater Road
Davison, Michigan
48423
info@ucanride.com

North American Riding for the Handicapped Association, Inc.
PO Box 33150 Denver,
Colorado 80233
NARHA@NARHA.ORG

United States Pony Clubs, INC
4041 Iron Works Parkway
Lexington, KY 40511
www.ponyclub.org

The American Horse Defense Fund
11206 Valley View Avenue
Kensington, MD 20895
www.ahdf.org

The American Horse Council
1616 H Street N.W. 7th Floor
Washington, DC 20006
(202) 296-4031
ahc@horsecouncil.org